Four Extra Hours

Creating the Life you Want
in the Time you Have

Jennifer Lynn O'Hara

ISBN-10: 0-9993738-0-3
ISBN-13: 978-0-9993738-0-4

This book is dedicated to everyone who has uttered the words, "If I only had more time."

ACKNOWLEDGMENTS

Big thanks go to….

Malinda, for being an inspiration.
Christina, for your amazing talent and generosity.
Steve, for always seeing the details.
And to all my friends and family who support me no matter what hair-brained idea I come up with.

CONTENTS

Art Galleries & Museums

Clock's Ticking...

1

INTRODUCTION & ORGANIZATION

Someone recently asked me what I would do if I had four extra hours in each week. I am sure they were trying to sell me some time saving gadget, but it got me thinking. What would I do if I magically found an additional four hours? And that sent my mind racing. Most questions of that nature are along the lines of, "What would you do if you won the lottery?" Or, "What would you do if you could travel anywhere in the world, and money was no obstacle?" But for most of us, those pie-in-the-sky questions are complete fantasy, and there's a billion-to-one chance we'll ever find ourselves in the position to make them a reality.

But four extra hours…that's different. That's do-able.

I will not try to deny that we are all busy. We have jobs, spouses, kids, and commitments. Life seems to move at warp speed, and it's getting faster every day. So how do we live the lives we want in the time we have? That is the big question. It seems impossible. We just don't have the time. Or do we?

Here's the thing... "I don't have time," is a myth. It's a lie that feels like the truth. Down deep in our souls, it feels like the god's-honest truth. But what if it's not? What if the truth is something we'd rather not face? Let's start by looking at the harsh reality of life.

The truth is that we're all given the same 24 hours in a day. No more, no less. Have you noticed that some people get so much done in a day while others seem to struggle with basic survival? Sure some people do have an advantage or disadvantage. Some people are born rich and some have to work two jobs just to make ends meet. Some people are single parents and some have no kids at all. But the majority of us only have one job, and most of us have kids and a family.

So what's the difference? How do those super-heroes accomplish so much while the rest of us labor endlessly with less-than-heroic results? The answer lies in how they treat their time and where they spend it.

The secret is to be intentional with the time we have. Those hypothetical four extra hours aren't going to magically fall into our laps. We have to work to make them happen. It's not about finding time, it's about making time. We must be intentional about how we spend our time, set boundaries, establish priorities, and – most importantly – ACT on them.

Time is our most valuable asset. Every minute that ticks by is a minute we're not getting back. So, whatever we do with it must be worth the price we pay. There is not a moment to waste. And if I had four extra hours a week – gosh, I could do a lot of things.

After that hypothetical question was posed to me I found myself making lists. Lists of "someday." Lists of dreams. Lists of people. And I could not sleep at night with all these lists forming and re-forming in my head. So to save my sanity and get some sleep, I decided to write them down. What resulted was this list of over 250 ideas of what to do with four extra hours in a week, and 12 time-saving tips to help make the time to do them.

I understand that most of us are in a position that, even if we could find four extra hours in a week, we would not be able to afford to do anything extravagant. So, while some of these ideas cost money, most are relatively cheap or free. There are no shopping sprees or impromptu trips to Europe on this list (although those would also be fun). This list contains only do-able things designed to enrich your life without emptying your bank account.

I've also included places to take notes and record your adventures as they happen. This can serve as a sort of diary as you work your way through the book. Hopefully these ideas and tips will inspire you to find the time to create the life you want to have.

2

TIME SAVING TIP #1

Get organized!

I wish I had some magical way to make four extra hours materialize out of nowhere. But unfortunately, there is no way to manufacture more than the 1,440 minutes a day we're already given. So how you manage that time is your magic key to getting four "extra" hours. The truth hurts: the people who get the most out of the time they're given are usually the most organized. I know – organization is not fun, or sexy, or exciting. It can be boring and monotonous. But it doesn't have to be an all-consuming endeavor that occupies every minute of your day. There are organizational apps such as 24me, IF, and many others that can make the job easier. And if you struggle with getting motivated or losing focus, try an app like 30/30, which turns your to-do list into a game and operates on the premise that most people can focus in 30 minute bursts and are more productive if they're being timed.

But what does "get organized" mean? It means different things to different people. The first step is to have an honest conversation with yourself and your loved ones and figure out where you are the most disorganized. Are you the kind to flit from one unfinished project to another? Are you a procrastinator who waits until the last minute to do everything? Or do you forget what needs to be done and spend more time catching up than getting ahead? We all have organizational weaknesses. The trick is to identify yours and take steps to fix it.

Start by tracking your time for a minimum of a week (longer is better). And I mean every minute. How many times do you hit the snooze button? How long do you stand in front of the closet deciding what to wear? How long does it take to make breakfast? You get the idea. An accurate picture of your starting point will show you what steps you need to take to reach your goal. Once you know that, make a plan. There are tools, like the apps mentioned earlier, but also calendaring techniques, electronic reminders, interactive list makers, and a whole host of other tools and resources to help you organize your life. Find the one (or ones) that work for you, make a plan and create a schedule, then STICK WITH IT and you'll be amazed at how much time you'll free up.

3

TIME SAVING TIP #2

Cook ahead!

It doesn't matter if you are a single person or a family with kids, we all struggle with finding time to prepare a home-cooked meal. But financial and nutritional experts alike agree that a home-cooked meal is usually healthier and more economical than most fast food options. The problem is finding the time to grocery shop and cook every day. No one has time for that.

The trick is to work ahead. Cook extra on Saturday or Sunday to prepare the bulk of your week's food items and have purposeful leftovers to make meals the rest of the week. It doesn't take that much longer to prepare larger amounts. And with a little strategic planning, you can have fast, healthy meals without the added time and expense of sitting in a drive-through line or eating out.

Rachael Ray even made a successful franchise out of it with her "Week in a Day" book and series. But savvy time-savers have been employing this technique for decades.

Start by making a menu for the week and buy your necessary ingredients. Plan your Day 1 meals, and then strategically plot out your leftover meals. Day 1 could be roast chicken, then plan a leftover meal of chicken quesadillas or chicken pot pie, etc. Your slow-cooker may become your new best friend. A good slow-cooker roast on Sunday could yield days of delicious leftover meals the next few days (shredded beef tacos, shepherd's pie, vegetable beef soup, etc.). And the beauty is that they won't taste like leftovers.

4

GO

The world is a great big place just waiting to be explored. Even as little as four hours a week will give you the time to explore places you've never been, or likely wouldn't normally have time to visit. You might not have time to fly somewhere, but four hours will certainly be enough time to do most of these things.

Drive

1. Pick a road on a map and see what's on it.

Ever wondered where Wandering Way goes? Or if there's a muffin shop on Drury Lane? Or if you could find Superman on Lois Lane? (Sorry about that last one – I couldn't resist.) A great way to get to know your town is to pick a road on a map and follow it to see where it goes. You never know, you might find your new favorite hole-in-the-wall eatery around the next corner.

My Adventure: _____

_____

_____

Date: _____

2. Pick an interesting sounding city and drive to it.

When I was little I loved *Charlotte's Web*. One day, while looking at a local map, we saw a town called Wilbur. Well, of course, we had to go. So we packed a lunch, piled in the car, and took a mini road-trip. That day is still one of my favorite days of childhood. Make your own adventure. Where will you go?

My Adventure: _____

_____

_____

Date: _____

3. Research local landmarks and actually visit.

Everyone's heard about Mt. Rushmore, the Statue of Liberty, or the Grand Canyon. But what about the Levi Coffin House? Or Boys Town? Or The Ringling? Local landmarks are everywhere, and their history can be as, or more, interesting than their more well-known cousins. Who knows, you might live right next to the world's biggest ball of aluminum foil. What local landmarks are near you?

My Adventure: _____

_____

_____

Date: _____

4. Do a "thrift store" hunt.

Sometimes the small mom-and-pop thrift stores are the least known, but have the best stuff. Because they don't belong to a national chain, they don't always have the advertising budget to do a full-scale marketing blitz. And that makes them the perfect hunting ground for savvy thrifters like you. Make a list of your favorite stores and add them to your visitation rotation.

My Adventure: _____

_____

_____

Date: _____

5. Go on a roll-the-dice adventure.

Grab a die or download a dice app. Roll it once, drive that many signals, roll again to determine right or left, then roll the die and go that many signals. Repeat the process a pre-determined number of rolls and see where you end up. Keep track of the interesting things you find, and where they're located, so you can visit them later.

My Adventure: _____

_____

_____

Date: _____

6. Explore a part of town you never get to during your normal routine.

If you live on the east side of town, take a few hours to visit the west. If you spend most of your time downtown, spend a day in the burbs. If we learned anything from *Footloose*, it's that sometimes the most fun can be found on the other side of the tracks. So break out of your neighborhood bubble, and see what other bubbles have to offer. Keep track of what you find.

My Adventure: _____

_____

_____

Date: _____

7. Plan a weekend road trip, and actually take it.

Maybe it's camping. Maybe it's a spa getaway. Or maybe it's just visiting friends who live the next town (or state) over. With four extra hours a week, you can afford to stretch your weekend plans into a road trip. A mini vacation may be just what you need to recharge those day-to-day batteries. Where could you go this weekend?

My Adventure: _____

_____

_____

Date: _____

8. Take your four-legged family members to the dog park.

Dogs get walked around their neighborhood all the time, and I'm sure it gets as boring for them as it does for us to see (and smell) the same things over and over again. So pile the pooches in the family truckster and drive on down to the local dog park. A little off-leash fun and canine socialization will be good for them (and you). Make a list of all the dog parks in your area.

My Adventure: _____

_____

_____

Date: _____

Walk

1. Walk around your neighborhood.

In this world of digital connectedness, we are even less connected than ever. Have you met your neighbors? Do you even know their names? Get a little exercise and strike up a conversation with your neighbor-down-the-street about her amazing rose garden. (Oh, and write their names down so you won't forget.)

My Adventure: _____

_____

_____

Date: _____

2. Explore downtown – even if it's small.

I live in a big town with a small town feel. Every city, big or small, has its charms, history, and a downtown district that is likely an interesting place to explore on foot. As the Petula Clark song says, "How can you lose? The lights are much brighter there, you can forget all your troubles, forget all your cares. So go downtown."

My Adventure: _____

_____

_____

Date: _____

3. Do a 3K or a 5K.

Kilometer walks/runs are a good thing on many levels. First, it's exercise, and who among us can do with less exercise? Second, it's a good opportunity to get out and hang with friends (and maybe meet new ones). Third, kilometer walk/runs usually benefit a worthy cause, so your participation is a win-win! Research local events and get out there and get walking.

My Adventure: _____

_____

_____

Date: _____

4. Mall walk.

If it's winter and you're in a cold climate, go to an indoor mall and start doing laps. Recruit some friends to stretch their legs with you. The great thing about walking in a mall in the winter is that it's light inside during the months when it's dark by 4pm outside. Oh, and there's no snow inside, so there's that. And bonus: you'll never miss out on a great sale.

My Adventure: _____

_____

_____

Date: _____

5. Go with a friend when he/she walks their dog.

I don't own a dog, but I have friends who do. And, while they absolutely love being puppy parents, sometimes the responsibility of walking them three times a day can get monotonous – especially if they walk them alone. So break that monotony and join them on a walk or two. Your friend will be thankful and the dogs will love having another person showering them with affection. Make a list of your friends with dogs and see if they'd like a little company.

My Adventure: _____
_____
_____

Date: _____

6. Take a nature walk.

Check the National Trail System to start your search for hiking trails in your area. There are too many trails to list on one site, so it might take a little cyber-sleuthing to find them all. But I promise they're worth checking out. Keep a list of the hard-to-find trails, and how to get there.

My Adventure: _____
_____
_____

Date: _____

7. Look online for self-guided historic walks.

Wikitravel is a good resource for this. As with most "Wiki" sights, the content is user-generated. If there's nothing for your area, do a little research and write/publish one yourself. You'll have fun in the process and provide a helpful resource for others to use. Keep a list of the historic areas you want to explore.

My Adventure: _____

_____

_____

Date: _____

8. Get a pedometer.

Set out in a different direction each day/week, and increase your daily/weekly step/distance goal as you continue to explore new places on every walk. If you're the competitive type, or the kind who likes to turn chores into games, a pedometer will give you the little boost of inspiration you need to get out there and get your steps in. Write your goals down so you can keep yourself accountable.

My Adventure: _____

_____

_____

Date: _____

Bike

1. To a local park.

You have the bike, but sometimes you lack a destination. That's where your local park comes in. Local parks usually offer good paths and pretty grounds. And bonus, parks often host events. So you just might stumble onto a concert or festival. Make a list of your local parks, and look online to see if there are any events scheduled.

My Adventure: _____

_____

_____

Date: _____

2. Along the river or coastline.

According to the National Oceanic and Atmospheric Administration there are over 95,000 miles of shoreline in the U.S. This number doesn't include smaller lakes, rivers, and creeks. With all this water, there is surely a waterside path perfect for a fun ride. Recruit a friend to go with you, and pack a picnic for a little riparian feast.

My Adventure: _____

_____

_____

Date: _____

3. Mountain bike.

If you live near a ski resort, you're in luck! Most ski resorts offer mountain-biking trails once the snow melts. Take the lift up, and ride the trails down. You get all the fun of mountain biking without the pesky peddling uphill. And if you don't live near a ski hub, you're not out of luck. The popularity of mountain biking has spurred cities, parks, and green-space managers to add bike paths. A quick online search should yield a list of them near you.

My Adventure: _____

_____

_____

Date: _____

4. To work.

May is National Bike Month, and an entire week in May is dedicated to biking to work. According to the League of American Bicyclists, 80% of the largest cities of the U.S. host Bike to Work events. And since as much as 40% of the everyday trips in the U.S. are an average of two miles, biking becomes a viable mode of transportation. Learn about Bike to Work events near you and participate.

My Adventure: _____

_____

_____

Date: _____

5. Find a designated bike path.

The popularity of biking has increased steadily over the past decade. And with the rise in popularity, cities and states are embracing the trend by including bike lanes, bike paths, and scenic bike tours as part of their road and park programs. There are hundreds of thousands of bike paths and trails across the country. So jump on the bicycling bandwagon, and claim a few miles for yourself.

My Adventure: _____

_____

_____

Date: _____

6. Get a bike rack for your car and explore towns, parks, etc.

As bicycling becomes more popular, the accompanying accessories get less expensive. If you're getting bored with your usual bike routes, invest in a bike rack and take your bike on a road trip. Explore miles of trails in a neighboring town or on the other side of that mountain range.

My Adventure: _____

_____

_____

Date: _____

7. Join a Meet-Up group for biking.

There are Meet-Up groups for just about everything – including bike-riding. Find one in your area and check them out. If you're nervous about riding with a bunch of strangers, recruit a friend to go with you the first few times. It's almost a guarantee you'll make new friends and feel comfortable attending solo in no time.

My Adventure: _____

_____

_____

Date: _____

8. Visit the local bike shop and ask about hidden-gem trails and bike groups.

The professionals at the bike shop probably don't work there for the million-dollar paycheck. They probably work there because they're passionate about cycling. And as experts, they probably have a lot of insights into the best places to ride, for every level and every area of interest. So take advantage of their knowledge and take the bike path less traveled.

My Adventure: _____

_____

_____

Date: _____

9. Peddle to the local farmer's market.

Buy a basket for your bike and visit the local farmer's market. Make sure your basket is the removable kind with a handle so you can carry it around the market. This is not only convenient, but will prevent you from buying more than you can safely carry home. (This is a voice of experience speaking.) Stock up on fresh produce for the week, and other goodies you may find. You're getting some exercise and helping support local farmers and merchants.

My Adventure: _____
_____
_____

Date: _____

Boat

1. Whale watching.

According to the NOAA over half of the American population lives within 50 miles of the coast. This means that whale watching opportunities are probably within easy reach. If you've never been whale watching, or have never seen a whale in the wild, you are missing one of life's most amazing experiences. If you haven't gone, go! If you have been, go again! Groupon and Living Social usually have great deals on whale watching adventures.

My Adventure: _____
_____
_____

Date: _____

2. Harbor cruise.

If open ocean cruises induce *Gilligan's Island* nightmares, perhaps a harbor cruise is more your speed. Harbor cruises are usually shorter and stay within sight of the shore. And bonus, they often come with a narrator who showcases the interesting points of interest along the way. Groupon and Living Social also offer great deals.

My Adventure: _____
_____
_____

Date: _____

3. River cruise.

If you're one of the less-than-fifty-percent of the population who does not live near the coast, don't fear – you won't be left high and dry. Nearly every river and lake has a business (or two or four) offering scenic river or lake cruises. The scenery is guaranteed to be beautiful and interesting, and you never know what kind of wildlife you'll see.

My Adventure: _____

_____

_____

Date: _____

4. Sunset dinner cruise.

Sunset cruises can be a romantic switch-up to your normal dating routine. But they are not limited to the purview of the romantically inclined. Sunset dinner cruises are also great options for a girls' night, a birthday party, or a reunion. There is something about being out on the water at that magic hour that makes the evening, well......magical.

My Adventure: _____

_____

_____

Date: _____

5. Speed boat.

There's nothing quite like the feeling of being on the water, with the wind in your hair, the sea spray in your face, and the throttle full forward to make you feel alive! Many touring and outrigging companies offer speed boat rides along the shore, lake, or river. So strap on your life jacket and get ready to have a ball!

My Adventure: _____

_____

_____

Date: _____

6. White water rafting.

Adrenaline junkies get in line, white water rafting is for you! If you're unsure, start small. Go in the fall, or on rivers that offer class II rapids. If you're an old pro at paddling the river waves, go with a tour company that tackles class III or IV. Rapids are rated by levels of difficulty from class I (Was that a bump?) to Class V (Holy sh**!).

My Adventure: _____

_____

_____

Date: _____

7. Canoeing or kayaking.

Kayaking is one of the most serene water activities I've ever experienced. Everything is at eye level, and from that vantage point you see things you might not otherwise notice...dragonflies flitting around the reeds, tiny fish glinting in the water, turtles along the shore. Go early in the morning to experience the sensation of gliding through the water silently as the rest of the world awakes.

My Adventure: _____

_____

_____

Date: _____

8. Peddle boats.

Many city parks with lakes offer peddle boats for rent. This aerobic exercise is cleverly disguised as a recreational activity. But despite its deceptive fitness trickery, peddle boats can be fun. Reliving childhood memories while getting a good leg tan can make you forget that you're actually exercising. And if exercising isn't your jam, go with a handsome hunk and let him do the heavy leg work.

My Adventure: _____

_____

_____

Date: _____

9. Take a sailing class.

Just read through the lyrics of Christopher Cross's song "Sailing," and you'll know why learning to sail can be your ticket to serenity. There's something miraculous about harnessing the power of the wind to move your vessel through the waves. The sea is a siren, and its song is as old as time. Its power has remained strong over the millennia for a reason, and millions of sailing-loving ancestors can't be wrong. Once you experience the sheer joy of sailing, you'll count yourself among those who are powerless against its pull. "Oh, the canvas can do miracles, just you wait and see…"

My Adventure: _____
_____
_____

Date: _____

Train

1. Scenic railways.

Hopping aboard a scenic train means you see country you would never get to see from the window of your car. The ruggedness and sheer beauty can be breathtaking. Many even feature a picturesque town at the end of the line, and ride-and-dine packages. Find a scenic railway in your neck of the woods and treat yourself to a trip.

My Adventure: _____
_____
_____

Date: _____

2. Narrow-gauge railways.

Train geeks…er, I mean enthusiasts…love narrow-gauge railways for their uniqueness and history. You'll love them for the same reasons. Narrow-gauge railways were built for industry, not passengers, so they go places people don't usually go. And because the cars are smaller they can go through country that is too rugged for standard cars.

My Adventure: _____
_____
_____

Date: _____

3. Historic trains.

Many trains have fascinating histories. Trains were the catalyst to taming the Wild West, the facilitator of industrialization, and the setting for some very interesting politics, romance, and intrigue. Because of the many juicy stories they have to tell, many rail lines offer history tours, which include narration, snacks, and even a recreation of historic events.

My Adventure: _____

_____

_____

Date: _____

4. Train museum.

One of Walt Disney's biggest loves was trains. Let's face it – trains bring out the kid in all of us. Why not treat the kid in you to a trip to your local train museum? Most even have small trains you can ride on and full-size cars you can climb in. And if you've ever wondered what it's like inside an engine or caboose, the train museum's the place to go. If you're not lucky enough to live near L.A. and see Walt's collection, look around your area for your local depot of train history.

My Adventure: _____

_____

_____

Date: _____

5. Amtrak to a neighboring town.

With names like Pacific Surfliner, Southwest Chief, and Texas Eagle, how could you not want to hop aboard and experience the luxury of a bygone era? The romance of the rails still calls, and those with adventurous hearts answer. But if you don't have the time or money to explore the country, why not explore the next town over? There's nothing like rocking with the rhythm of the rails.

My Adventure: _____

_____

_____

Date: _____

6. Do a mystery dinner theater train experience.

Some trains offer nights of entertainment, with food, music, or a floor show that travels from car to car. And if you're really lucky, you live in an area where local actors put on a murder mystery show. It would be like *Murder on the Orient Express*, except without traveling overseas, or spending a gazillion dollars, or huge snow drifts. So not really like *Murder on the Orient Express* at all, but still cool.

My Adventure: _____

_____

_____

Date: _____

7. Take the town trolley for a spin.

If your town has a trolley or hop-on/hop-off bus, take it to see things from a tourist's eyes. Most local trolleys and sight-seeing buses have ongoing narration. It's fun to see the same old place from a fresh new perspective. And I can almost promise you'll learn something you didn't know before you boarded.

My Adventure: _____

_____

_____

Date: _____

8. At Christmas, take the Santa Train.

In almost every major city, there is usually a Santa Train during the holidays. Most employ people who dress up as elves, invite riders to dress in the most festive attire, and ride a special train that ends at the "North Pole" to visit Santa. Even if you don't have kids, appeal to the kid in you, put on your best ugly Christmas sweater, board the Santa Train, and revel in the magic of the season.

My Adventure: _____

_____

_____

Date: _____

5

TIME SAVING TIP #3

Plan your wardrobe!

I shudder to think how much time I've wasted standing paralyzed in front of my closet every day. Some research has shown that people, particularly women, can spend as much as one year of their life picking out clothes. One year! That's a lot of time staring at my wardrobe.

I have a closet full of clothes, but can never seem to find anything to wear. And in my rush to get out the door every morning, my decision-making skills are significantly hindered. So I waste time and end up making bad fashion choices – all because I didn't do a little wardrobe pre-planning.

Plan your wardrobe for the week, even if it's just in your head. Each Sunday, map out what you're going to wear to work each day that week, and make sure it's all clean/pressed. Then hang your pre-chosen outfits on one side of your closet, so they're easy to grab and throw on. Sure, there will be days when you change your mind. But most days you'll be thankful you spared yourself the pain of suffering wardrobe paralysis. There are even great apps, like Stylebook, that will allow you to take pics of the items in your closet, then use those pics to make outfits. Bonus: this will also save time when you're out shopping to help you buy only what you need, and what will fit into your existing wardrobe.

6

TIME SAVING TIP #4

Clean as you go!

In my early working years I held jobs in a number of food service businesses. They all had two mantras they recited regularly: "Clean as you go," and, "If you have time to lean, you have time to clean." Of course, these were restaurant settings, where people were being paid by the hour, so of course they wanted their employees to be using that time wisely. But is your time at home any less valuable than that of restaurant staff? The secret here is that it takes far less time to clean as you go than to let everything pile up and then try to tackle a seemingly insurmountable mountain of cleaning chores. So resist the urge to pile all the dirty dishes in the sink. Instead, get in the habit of rinsing and putting dishes in the dishwasher immediately (or washing and putting away if you don't have a dishwasher), and you'll never face a sink overflowing with dirty dishes again. The same goes for mail. Go through mail and process it every day instead of throwing it in a pile until it becomes an overwhelming task to sort through.

Getting into a routine also helps save time. If you need help, try an app like Home Routines, which allows you to input common household tasks and put them on a schedule to be done. It then sends you reminders to actually do them. It also breaks the house into zones to make cleaning more efficient.

7

DO

How many times have we all said, "If I only had a little extra time I'd…"? Those words are the death of our adventurous spirit. So, make some extra time, get off the couch, and DO some of those things on your "someday" list. Or, do some of the things listed in this section. There's something here for everyone – and everything here is virtually promised to enrich your life.

Cultural

1. Visit a museum or two.

Everyone's heard of the big museums: the Getty, the Smithsonian, the Met. But what about the smaller museums? When I was in Dublin recently, I had the good fortune to stumble upon The Little Museum of Dublin. And that's exactly what it was: little. It was essentially a house-turned-museum, but it was one of the coolest museums I've ever been to. Sure, small, local museums probably won't be able to host a huge Monet exhibit. But what they do showcase is often just as interesting, and often much more intimate and far less crowded. Don't forego the big museums – they are spectacular. But don't overlook the small ones either. Make a list of all the big and small museums in your area and pay them a visit.

My Adventure: _____

_____

_____

Date: _____

2. Go to the symphony.

No, really – go to the symphony! Many people see the symphony as a high-brow, high-culture night of boring music from long-dead white guys. But that's not always true! In my area, one orchestra put on a concert of music from popular video games. Another symphony showcased music from John Williams. (You know, the guy who composed music for *Star Wars* and *Indiana Jones* and *Superman* and *E.T.* and *Jaws*…yeah, THAT guy.) And yet another symphony presented a slate of classical music featured in cartoons, and played the accompanying cartoons on a giant screen. Boring, you say? I think it's time to take another look at the symphony.

My Adventure: _____

_____

_____

Date: _____

3. See the ballet.

OK, this one may be a hard sell to some. But the ballet has changed over the decades, and is not always the stuffy, sleep-inducing event many fear it will be, especially if you know the stories behind the ballets. Most of the classic ballets are based on fascinating stories. A little research into the story ahead of time will make the ballet come to life in ways it never did before. And many ballet companies are modernizing their repertoire with current dance styles and music, which appeal to a younger crowd. So, do yourself a favor and give the ballet a chance.

My Adventure: _____

_____

_____

Date: _____

4. Take in a lecture.

Lectures and learning opportunities can be found in unexpected places. Health lectures are hosted at hospitals and medical centers. Speaker's series can be seen at performing arts centers. Academic lectures and debates are held at local colleges. Wildlife and nature lectures can be enjoyed at aquariums and nature centers. View TED Talks online. Whatever your interest, there is likely a speech or lecture or presentation near you.

My Adventure: _____

_____

_____

Date: _____

5. Enjoy wine (or brew) tasting.

Artisanal wineries and craft breweries are popping up all over, and most of them have tasting rooms to showcase their products to potential buyers. Go on a self-guided wine tasting tour with a designated driver, or sign up for a guided tour and leave the driving to a professional.

My Adventure: _____

_____

_____

Date: _____

6. Visit art galleries or attend an opening.

Art galleries change their exhibits often, and when they do, they usually host an opening reception. It's fun to put on your snazzy clothes and enjoy hors d'oeuvres while staring at canvases with a vaguely knowing look on your face. If you've missed the opening, put on your everyday clothes and enjoy the art anyway. Go to a martini bar after to complete the cultured, cosmopolitan effect.

My Adventure: _____

_____

_____

Date: _____

7. Join local cultural groups.

If you're Irish (or other nationality), join the Irish (or other nationality) Network. You'll meet new people and participate in fun and interesting events. If language is your thing, join a language club. Or, if you have the travel bug, join a travel group filled with like-minded global wanderers. But here's the important thing – even if you're NOT Irish, or don't speak another language, or haven't yet traveled, joining groups with different cultural focuses will give you the gift of a broader perspective.

My Adventure: _____

_____

_____

Date: _____

8. Join local specialty groups.

There are guilds and clubs and groups and organizations of every type and sort out there. Enjoy quilting? Join a quilt guild. Want to save the environment? Join an environmental group. You get the idea. Whatever your interest, there's a group out there for you. It might take a little digging to find one to suit your interests, but I can almost guarantee there's at least one group (and probably more) just waiting for you to join their ranks.

My Adventure: _____

_____

_____

Date: _____

9. Join a book club.

Reading is one of those guilty-pleasure activities I have a hard time justifying. Yet reading is also one of the best things you can do to keep your mind sharp, to increase knowledge, and exercise your imagination. So why not join a book club? You'll have a justification (read: excuse) to put your feet up and dig into a good book guilt-free.

My Adventure: _____

_____

_____

Date: _____

Sports

1. Go to a football/baseball/hockey/whatever game.

Even if you don't live in a town with a major league team, you can still enjoy sportsing by checking out the Triple-A or Double-A teams. Or support your local college or high school team. *Friday Night Lights* didn't become a thing for nothing. There's something wholesome about farm-team games. And that's so very Americana.

My Adventure: _____

_____

_____

Date: _____

2. Join a softball league.

I will be the first to admit I am the world's worst softball player. But being on a team is actually kinda fun. The trick is to find the right team. If you're like me (and I know I am), you need to be on a team where everyone plays as badly as you, and where no one cares if you win or lose. If I set out with the intention of fun, not victory, I can relax and laugh at myself. So go on, people – get out there and suck!

My Adventure: _____

_____

_____

Date: _____

3. Go bowling.

The only thing I'm worse at than softball is bowling. As of this writing, I have never broken 100. Pretty bad, huh? But when I go with friends, it's not about the score. It's about eating bowling alley food, drinking watered down margaritas, wearing those oh-so-groovy shoes, and laughing 'til our faces hurt. And if we happen to knock down a pin or two along the way, yay us!

My Adventure: _____

_____

_____

Date: _____

4. Practice archery.

Archery…the sport of ages past. The romanticized weapon of Robin Hood and nearly every historical fiction romance novel ever written. The favorite activity of every summer camp. But why relegate archery to books or childhood? There are plenty of public archery ranges. And in no time at all you, too, can be reliving those carefree days of Camp Winnemehokkahfinnumepookee.

My Adventure: _____

_____

_____

Date: _____

5. Try your hand at trap/skeet shooting.

OK, this one's a little controversial, because…guns. But let's step aside from the 2nd Amendment debate for now and look at shooting as a sport. The kind you do at the Olympics. Trap/skeet shooting is actually fun. Most ranges have gun rentals and pros to help you get started. So step out of your comfort zone and give it a try.

My Adventure: _____

_____

_____

Date: _____

6. Go horseback riding.

Ahhhh….my favorite. Even before I could say the word "horse" I was infatuated. They were my first love, and still have the power to steal my heart with one look. Every time I'm on the back of a horse, the rest of the world melts away, my soul is at peace, and all is well. Most larger cities have riding stables that rent by the hour, and have a variety of horses for riders of all levels. So if you've never ridden, do yourself a favor and go. If you're an avid rider, do yourself a favor and go again.

My Adventure: _____

_____

_____

Date: _____

7. Learn to surf or paddleboard.

Surfing, I'm told, is addictive. I've never been able to get past my fear of sharks to try it (cue the *Jaws* music), but others tell me it's quite the spiritual experience. Paddleboarding, likewise, is a fun activity that can also be done in lakes as well as the ocean, and is a good form of exercise, with a less-steep learning curve.

My Adventure: _____

_____

_____

Date: _____

8. Learn to scuba.

Scuba is an incredible way to explore the undersea universe. But you can't just strap on a tank and jump in – it takes lessons, practice, schooling, and testing to ensure you don't meet an early demise. (Unless you get eaten by a shark. But that's another issue entirely.) If you're a guy, being able to scuba dive makes you look cool. If you're a girl, the male/female ratio among scuba divers is in your favor. So there are lots of great reasons to learn to scuba.

My Adventure: _____

_____

_____

Date: _____

9. Go snorkeling.

Snorkeling is a good alternative to the sometimes-expensive hobby of scuba diving. With snorkeling, you don't need super-expensive equipment or special training to get started. With some basic equipment, and a few YouTube tutorials, you can be on your way to enjoying the underwater views.

My Adventure: _____

_____

_____

Date: _____

10. Take a hike.

There is no shortage of hiking trails in this great nation. And if you don't have specific trails near you, I bet you have country roads, or scenic neighborhoods, or something similar. How many have you walked? Even in my little corner of the world, I have only taken a fraction of the trails available to me. I could go on and on with study after study about the physical and mental health benefits of walking, and exercise, and being outside, and fresh air and sunshine. But you already know all that.

My Adventure: _____

_____

_____

Date: _____

11. Learn to golf.

I thought I'd try to be all highfalutin and learn to play golf, so I took golf lessons at a local Nike Golf School (thank you, Groupon!). It was actually fun (and the golf pros were adorable). I gotta tell ya – it made all the difference when I play mini-golf. Now I SKUNK those six-year-olds! They never know what hit 'em.

My Adventure: _____

_____

_____

Date: _____

12. Check out your Parks & Recreation department.

Your local Parks & Rec office is a great resource for sports leagues, classes, and events. These resources are paid for by your tax dollars, so use them! The people who work there have jobs because their services are utilized. So get out there, and get active!

My Adventure: _____

_____

_____

Date: _____

Entertainment

1. Attend a music festival.

There are so many music festivals to suit every musical taste. You don't have to wait for the giant Coachellas or Lollapaloozas of the world to enjoy a good music festival. There are plenty of smaller music festivals to enjoy. And music festivals usually include other activities, like food booths, shopping, and wine/beer tasting.

My Adventure: _____

_____

_____

Date: _____

2. Explore a Renaissance faire.

Geek out at your local Renaissance Faire (or "Ren Faire" if you're a true geek). Sure, you can go all medieval and dress the part. But most people I know go in regular 21st century attire. It's fun to take a step back in time, enjoy Ren Faire food, kitschy entertainment, and hand-crafted art. So, good sir, lay hand on ye olde turkey leg, and attend the faire!

My Adventure: _____

_____

_____

Date: _____

3. Go to the theater.

Let's get this straight. When I say "theater," I don't mean a multiplex. I mean an actual stage, with live actors, and a three-dimensional set. Yeah, THAT kind of theater. Just like the symphony, today's theater is not exclusively for the high-brow blue-hair set. Today's plays deal with modern themes and use everyday language. Musicals include rap and grunge and soul and hip-hop music. So treat yourself to a new cultural experience.

My Adventure: _____
_____
_____

Date: _____

4. A night at the movies.

One of the first things that gets cut when we're busy is entertainment time. With four extra hours, you'll have time to fit in a movie here and there. The experience of seeing a film on the big screen can't quite be duplicated at home. So take a 2-hour mental vacation and go! You have four extra hours, so what's stopping you?

My Adventure: _____
_____
_____

Date: _____

5. Visit the county fair.

As a little girl, one of the things I looked forward to most was the county fair. There was nothing more magical than a huge carnival combined with barn after barn of noisy animals, arts & crafts, food, concerts, and all manner of shopping. As an adult, the magic hasn't faded. In fact, I take my four extra hours a week to drive to neighboring counties to attend their fairs. You can never have too many elephant ears or roasted corn-on-the-cob.

My Adventure: _____

_____

_____

Date: _____

6. Rock out at a concert.

Channel your inner head-banger and attend a concert. I am *mumblemumble* years old, and just attended my first U2 concert. It's never too late to go! Soak in the communal experience of hearing iconic bands live. The energy of a live concert is not something that can be explained adequately in words; it must be experienced.

My Adventure: _____

_____

_____

Date: _____

7. Support a local band.

Small venues, bars, and coffee shops often host local bands. It's a great way to support local musicians or see a band before they become the next big thing. I and a group of my friends enjoyed seeing this quirky band with a goofy name who played fun songs, so we would see them often...always in small venues. Today, the world knows them as Barenaked Ladies.

My Adventure: _____

_____

_____

Date: _____

8. Spend the day at an amusement park.

So you don't live near Disneyland? So what! The world does not live on Disney alone. (Please forgive me, Disney. I still love you.) I have traveled all around the world and have seen amusement parks in the most unlikely of places. Visit Dollywood in Tennessee, Elitch Gardens in Denver, Cedar Point in Ohio, Silverwood in Northern Idaho, just to name a few.

My Adventure: _____

_____

_____

Date: _____

9. Get an ab workout at a comedy club.

One of my favorite things to do is to spend an evening at the comedy club. Laughter is the best medicine, and a comedy club provides a healthy dose. Many clubs feature "headliner" nights, with celebrity comedians. But often their regular nights of lesser known acts are as funny (and usually cheaper). Either way, it's a good night out.

My Adventure: _____

_____

_____

Date: _____

10. Explore the local strawberry/tomato/garlic/corn festival.

The close cousin of the county fair is the *insert generic produce here* festival. Gilroy, CA has its garlic festival. Swanton, OH has its corn festival. Fruita, CO has its Mike The Headless Chicken festival. (This is true. You can't make this stuff up.) Doubtless there are countless fill-in-the-blank festivals near you. They are fun. They are kitschy. They are worth your four extra hours.

My Adventure: _____

_____

_____

Date: _____

Cuisine

1. Hole-in-the-wall list from the local paper or magazine.

About a decade ago my local paper published a list of 75 hole-in-the-wall restaurants you shouldn't miss. My friends and I decided to make it our mission to visit them all. Slowly, week-by-week, we worked our way through the list. Along the way we found some new favorite eats, some places we didn't like so much, and had a lot of fun. Create your own adventure!

My Adventure: _____

_____

_____

Date: _____

2. *Diners, Drive-Ins, & Dives* locations.

If you're a Food Network addict like me, you've seen your share of *Diners, Drive-Ins, & Dives*. I've eaten at a few of those joints, and they make Guy's list for a reason. Be brave and try the menu items featured on the show.

My Adventure: _____

_____

_____

Date: _____

3. Top user-generated lists.

I've found that most user-generated lists, such as Yelp & Trip Advisor, etc., are pretty spot-on. Sure, you'll have your share of detractors who want one business to fail only so another can win. Or who rank a place low because the parking was challenging (not a fair review, in my opinion). But for the most part, those lists have guided me to some amazing eateries I would have never found on my own.

My Adventure: _____

_____

_____

Date: _____

4. Resort hotel restaurants.

Fancy hotel restaurants may be cost-prohibitive to visit for a full meal at peak times. But the same fancy restaurants are much more affordable (and less busy) at lunch time. Or, stop in for dessert and coffee/tea. This is a good way to try the platinum restaurants on an aluminum budget.

My Adventure: _____

_____

_____

Date: _____

5. Foreign flavors.

Make a list of all the regional/ethnic foods you've never tried, and then find a list of restaurants that offer them. Ever tried Ethiopian food? Creole? Indonesian? Nicaraguan? Now's your chance! Take your four extra hours and start tasting.

My Adventure: _____

_____

_____

Date: _____

6. Coffee house tour.

Coffee houses don't serve just coffee. They also serve artisanal or home-made pastries and snacks, and many of them serve full meals. Because they're small-batch and usually upscale or trendy, coffee house cuisine can be a real treat.

My Adventure: _____

_____

_____

Date: _____

7. Gastro pubs.

Unlike your traditional fish-and-chips pub, gastro pubs specialize in high-quality food. And usually it's unique and chef-created. Gastro pubs are the new "it" place to gather and partake in delicious food, delicious drinks, and delicious conversation.

My Adventure: _____

_____

_____

Date: _____

8. Go on a picnic.

The sweet innocence of a picnic is as fun for adults as it is for kids. As adults, we don't go on picnics often enough, and that's a shame. Sure, it takes a little time to pack the lunch, travel to the park, and set up your feast. But the fresh air, sunshine, and connection with the outdoors are certainly worth the effort. Take a good book to complete your escape.

My Adventure: _____

_____

_____

Date: _____

9. Throw a dinner party.

"Dinner party" conjures images of 1960s businessmen and their fashionably-clad wives carrying martinis around a mid-century modern home. But today's dinner parties aren't nearly as stuffy. Throw a theme party and plan your food accordingly. Host a costume party. Make finger foods and have a game night. Have a 1960s throwback party. The point is to have friends over for food and fun. Voila! A dinner party.

My Adventure: _____

_____

_____

Date: _____

10. Invite friends for a potluck dinner.

Make it a "take and share" event, where people bring their favorite dishes and then trade recipes. Obviously you'll have to set some guidelines to prevent there being eight kinds of desserts, but no main dishes or sides. But with some basic organization, you'll have a delicious version of show-and-tell, and a fun evening with friends.

My Adventure: _____

_____

_____

Date: _____

11. Invite friends to go out to dinner.

Instead of going to your favorite place, take them to their favorite place. Make a plan to never visit the same place twice, and see where the whims of fate and friends lead you. You never know what culinary treasures you'll find.

My Adventure: _____

_____

_____

Date: _____

Home

1. Get out in the garden.

Gardening isn't restricted to homeowners. Apartment dwellers can garden, too. Most apartments I've rented have had some sort of balcony, and that's a perfect place for a container garden. If you don't have a balcony, try some indoor gardening by planting herbs in a window sill.

My Adventure: _____
_____
_____

Date: _____

2. Tackle a DIY.

Let your inner HGTV diva shine by tackling a little DIY. If you're new to DIY don't jump into the deep end right away. Save things that could cause fire or death to the professionals. Start with things that won't cause loss of life or limb, like recovering those old dining room chairs. Or upcycle an old pallet into rustic wall art. There are how-to videos on YouTube for just about anything.

My Adventure: _____
_____
_____

Date: _____

3. Get your craft on.

Crafting is both therapeutic and brain-stimulating. And there are so many types of crafting available these days, there is bound to be something to suit every taste. Wander through your local craft store to get inspiration, or attend a class.

My Adventure: _____

_____

_____

Date: _____

4. Deep clean.

There are so many tasks in our homes that have been put on the "when I have time" list. But, since most of us are busier than we've ever been, the "I have time" time never comes. So, the windows never get washed, the floor under the couch (or refrigerator or stove or bed) never gets swept or vacuumed, the tiny space behind the toilet continues to gather dust. Use your four extra hours to do all those tasks and take them off the blackhole of to-do lists.

My Adventure: _____

_____

_____

Date: _____

5. Paint the walls.

Painting is the biggest (and cheapest) bang for your home-improvement buck. You can change the look of an entire room by painting one wall. Or, go whole-hog and paint the entire room. Don't be afraid to get creative. It's only paint. The worst that can happen is that you have to paint over it.

My Adventure: _____

_____

_____

Date: _____

6. Cook real food.

The biggest reason people give for opting for the drive-through is "not enough time to cook." With four extra hours you'll have plenty of time! And if it still doesn't feel like it, start with the many 30- or 16-minute meal recipes out there. There are literally thousands of them. Also, be sure to check out the cooking section of the "Time Saving Tips" to learn how to make home-cooked meals without spending hours slaving over a stove.

My Adventure: _____

_____

_____

Date: _____

7. Organize those catch-all drawers and files.

Everyone has one. Don't deny it. It's an inevitability of not being a nomad. A junk drawer isn't necessarily bad. Where else can you store all those gadgets and gizmos a-plenty? Stop fighting it – organize it. A junk drawer stops being a junk drawer when it's organized. Take everything out, go through it, throw away, sort, organize, then buy a drawer organizer to tame the junk madness.

My Adventure: _____

_____

_____

Date: _____

8. Finally get caught up on laundry.

Remember those *Flintstone* cartoons where Fred munches on a giant drumstick, and no matter how many bites he takes, the drumstick never gets smaller? That's what laundry feels like. It would be wonderful to have extra time to get it all done and just sit back for 10 minutes and revel in the knowledge that there isn't a single thing that needs to be laundered. Ahhhh....the simple joys.

My Adventure: _____

_____

_____

Date: _____

9. Binge the latest Netflix sensation.

It may be a guilty pleasure, but with four extra hours, there is less guilt in binge watching your latest Netflix (or Amazon, or Hulu, or HBO) addiction. So pop some popcorn, grab your favorite blankie, and make a nest in your couch. Don't worry, I won't judge.

My Adventure: _____

_____

_____

Date: _____

10. Go through closets and cupboards.

Do a major clean-out of things you don't use anymore. Be brutally honest! You may eventually lose those pesky 40 pounds, but don't save all those size 4s you can't wear now. Donate them to a local charity and treat yourself to new clothes as a reward for dropping the weight. You deserve it!

My Adventure: _____

_____

_____

Date: _____

11. Rearrange a room.

It's easy to get complacent with our living spaces. The home I just bought had not been updated since the 1970s, and let me tell you, the '70s were not kind to interior decorating. Rearranging a room can breathe new life into your living space and help you see it in a different light. You may fall in love with a piece all over again. Or, you may realize that your harvest gold shag couch no longer fits your style ethic.

My Adventure: _____

_____

_____

Date: _____

12. Redecorate on a dime.

I love those design-for-cheap and upcycle shows. Take their tips to heart and refurbish and repurpose hidden treasures. A coat of paint does wonders for a 1980s bookcase. Some artfully decoupaged drawer fronts can hide an otherwise past-repair chest of drawers. Some re-decorators have turned their hobby into a profit-making venture. With four extra hours, what can you do?

My Adventure: _____

_____

_____

Date: _____

Jennifer Lynn O'Hara

8

TIME SAVING TIP #5

Watch your social media usage!

I know, I know...I love my social media, too. It's how we stay connected, network, learn what's going on in the world, sell our products, etc., etc., etc. But there comes a time when our social media usage outpaces our actual human interaction and completely obliterates our productivity. When that happens, it's time to fight fire with fire. There are several apps that will help you bring your digital addiction under control. It might seem odd to use an app in an effort to lessen the time you use apps. But here's the problem: people severely underestimate the amount of time they spend on their phones and tablets, specifically using social media. Recent meta-analysis shows that people are spending as much as seven hours per day on their phones or tablets looking at social media. Seven hours! Per day! So a wake-up call to your true addiction level may be required.

There are a lot of helpful apps out there, but here are two of my favorites. The QualityTime app keeps track of how many times a phone is unlocked each day, (some studies show the average is 150 times per day), and how much time is spent on each site/app, so you can keep track of both frequency and duration. You can generate reports and graphs, and see a true picture of the time you spend on your digital device. And if you truly are a digital addict, an app like BreakFree might be for you. BreakFree not only monitors your digital habits, but sends you notifications when usage is heavy. It can also be set to disable certain aspects of your phone/tablet's usage when a specified threshold has been met, or turn off sounds and notifications during family time or other events.

9

TIME SAVING TIP #6

Become a morning person!

Right now all my night-owl friends are groaning and rolling their eyes. I've been a morning person all my life and have always espoused the merits of getting up early. My friends and family have endured a lifetime of me being happy and energetic and singing in the morning, while they're hating everyone and everything that makes noise before 10am. Sorry folks, but the research is on my side. Behavioral scientists have done productivity studies that show the most productive hours are in the morning.

Don't believe me? Look it up. *The Wall Street Journal* even reported on their findings. Productivity and efficiency are higher in the morning and decline steadily after lunch. Now, here's the caveat: everyone is different and everyone has their own "most productive" hours.

But the majority of people, according to the studies, are more productive in the morning hours, whether they want to admit to it or not. I can hear all you night-owls saying, "Well, I'm in that minority of people who are more productive at night." Sorry again, you can't all be in the minority, otherwise you'd be the majority. So, it's time to face facts – as much as you may hate it, getting up earlier may help you be more productive, efficient, and effective, thereby saving time.

And since we're talking about facts, here's one for you. If you got up just one hour earlier every day, you'd gain an extra fifteen days in a year. Fifteen days! It's kinda hard to wrap your mind around that, isn't it? Now doesn't that sound a whole lot more appealing than hitting the snooze button?

Oh, and once you start becoming a morning person, try to skip the mindless tasks and social media nonsense until after lunch. Save those precious productive/efficient hours for the most important things that need your full attention.

10

LEARN

Learning doesn't have to end when you graduate from high school or college. Learning should be a lifelong endeavor. Studies have shown over and over again that continuing learning boosts brain power and staves off memory-related diseases. And learning opportunities are everywhere. Your local community college is a resource – it's cheap and you don't have to be a "real" student to take classes. Other venues that are not normally associated with classes, like museums, art galleries, and community centers, often offer great classes and lectures at very reasonable prices.

Community College

1. Dance.

Ever wanted to learn to tap? Or take a cue from *Dancing with the Stars* and learn some old-school ballroom? Dance classes at a traditional studio can be prohibitively expensive. But classes through your local community college are super cheap, and taught by legit professionals. This semester I'm taking African Dance, next semester...who knows?

My Adventure: _____

_____

_____

Date: _____

2. Paint.

Bob Ross is one of my heroes. He brought painting to the masses and showed the world how easy it is to paint "happy little trees." He took the fear out of painting, which gave me the confidence to try it myself. I took a few classes at my local community college and at a local nature center, and then I was off and running. My house is now filled with my own work. Bob would be proud.

My Adventure: _____

_____

_____

Date: _____

3. History.

After watching a few episodes of *Reign* and *The Crown*, I wanted to learn the "real" story of these larger-than-life characters. So I turned my latest Netflix binge into real learning and took a history class. You can, too. There's nothing like a good professor to make the subject come alive. And since you would be attending for fun, and not for grades, there's no pressure to ace that mid-term.

My Adventure: _____

_____

_____

Date: _____

4. Writing.

The next Great American Novel could be at the end of your fingertips. Take that great idea living in your brain and put it on paper. Don't think too much about it – just start writing. If you're the structured type, write an outline first, then connect the dots with narrative. A class on creative writing will give you oodles of instruction. So take your four extra hours and start writing.

My Adventure: _____

_____

_____

Date: _____

5. Technology.

It doesn't matter what age you are, there is a technology deficit in your life somewhere. Whether it's wishing you knew more about graphic design or programming, or whether you're a tech prodigy or a newbie, there is a community college class out there for you. With a little knowledge, technology can be your friend.

My Adventure: _____

_____

_____

Date: _____

6. Sports.

I wanted to learn to play golf. I don't know why – I just got a wild hair one day. So I signed up for a golf class. The golf professor was very good and within a few weeks I actually looked like I knew what I was doing. If golf isn't your thing try another sport. It doesn't have to become a lifelong passion, the fun is in the learning.

My Adventure: _____

_____

_____

Date: _____

7. Pottery.

Live out your inner Patrick Swayze *Ghost* fantasy and enroll in a pottery class. You'll likely start with hand-formed pieces, but will move up to the wheel where you get to "throw" your own projects. And community colleges already have all the equipment –you just pay a small usage fee. This is one of those crafts that isn't yet widely practiced, so you'll have a supply of one-of-a-kind Christmas and birthday gifts whenever you need them. Or, turn your new hobby into a money-making venture.

My Adventure: _____
_____
_____

Date: _____

8. Public speaking.

Many studies have shown that public speaking ranks near the top of people's lists of things that terrify them – even outranking death in many cases. Conquer that fear by enrolling in a public speaking course. It could be formal, like a college class. Or less formal, like a Toastmasters group. Don't let fear stop you – to my knowledge, no one has dropped dead from fear of public speaking.

My Adventure: _____
_____
_____

Date: _____

9. Music.

Most people learn instruments as children. And while it's easier to learn when you're a kid, it's not impossible to learn as adults. There are an endless number of music classes available in any format and venue you want. Guitar is probably the cheapest and easiest to grasp. But if you've ever wanted to learn the tuba or bagpipes or harp – don't waste a minute, get to it.

My Adventure: _____

_____

_____

Date: _____

10. Car repair.

Ever wonder how much of a sales job you're getting when you take your car to the shop? Take the guess work out of car repairs and take a class. I'm not suggesting you try to refurbish your car's transmission yourself. But a little basic knowledge of what happens under the hood may be able to help you decide if you're being fed a line of bull at the auto shop.

My Adventure: _____

_____

_____

Date: _____

11. Language.

The U.S. has fallen behind other countries in language programs. Sure, we're given language classes as an elective in high school, and as requirements in college. But other nations require much more, and their students graduate speaking two or three languages. Apps like Duolingo are fantastic for learning the basics, but they lack the kind of conversational experience you can get in a classroom setting.

My Adventure: _____

_____

_____

Date: _____

12. Literature.

Literature isn't just about literature. It's also about history, creative writing, social anthropology, and myriad other things wrapped into one academic subject. If you have a specific interest, enroll in classes geared toward that topic. There are classes focusing on 20th Century works, romantic works, medieval writers, even literature through classic horror novels. Find one that tickles your literary fancy and get reading.

My Adventure: _____

_____

_____

Date: _____

13. Cosmetology/Aesthetician.

This one may seem a bit "out there" for most people. But knowing the science behind skin care products can help you decide what you do, and do not, want to put on your skin. Learning the "why" behind the what and how can help you understand what product labels are really saying. And who knows, you may even formulate your own cosmetic line and become a billionaire!

My Adventure: _____

_____

_____

Date: _____

Library

1. Attend author readings/signings.

Many libraries offer author book signings and readings. If you've never heard a book read by the author's own voice, you don't know what you're missing. Usually the author has insights into the book that resonate in their voice. It's also a great way to support local authors and artists.

My Adventure: _____

_____

_____

Date: _____

2. Summer reading programs.

My local library has a summer reading program. The structure is fairly loose – read a certain amount of books in a certain amount of time, and do some associated activities. You do get some swag for completing the program. But the real benefit is reading and participating and supporting your local library.

My Adventure: _____

_____

_____

Date: _____

3. Check out a book and actually read it.

I have checked out so many books with the best of intentions. But, nary a page gets read before I have to return them. Now that I have four extra hours, I actually have time to read the books (or, at least most of them) before I have to return them.

My Adventure: _____

_____

_____

Date: _____

4. Rent DVDs and CDs.

One of the things many people don't know is that libraries check out more than just books. Most also check out DVDs and CDs. So if your favorite film isn't Netflix streamable, and you don't want to wait for the DVD to arrive in the mail – check it out from your local library. Some larger libraries also check out other things as well. The library where I grew up used to check out artwork, and it was fun having a rotating display of original oils on my walls at all times.

My Adventure: _____

_____

_____

Date: _____

5. Read newspapers and magazines.

Save money on subscriptions and read magazines at the library. Your local library likely carries the most popular titles, plus many you've probably never heard of. It's a great way to "test drive" a magazine to see if you want to subscribe before parting with your dough.

My Adventure: _____

_____

_____

Date: _____

6. "Borrow" free ebooks.

Libraries have gone hi-tech, and you can "check out" books for your e-reader. Don't ask me how they do it because that kind of magic is beyond me. But I've seen it happen, so I know it's real. And they have more than just books. Check out the other tools and resources available for your e-reader – all check-out-able online.

My Adventure: _____

_____

_____

Date: _____

7. Take a course offered by the library.

Many libraries offer classes and lectures. Usually they're literary related, and they're often free or very inexpensive. I am a Jane Austen fan, and recently went to a library-sponsored function featuring an expert in 18th Century food and dining rituals. It was fascinating to understand the social constructs behind Austen's writing. Because of that class, her books got better; not because her writing improved, but because I understood it more fully.

My Adventure: _____

_____

_____

Date: _____

8. Book sale!

Browse the library book sale for hidden gems. Periodically, libraries have book sales to clean out their shelves, rid themselves of multiple copies, or replace older copies with newer versions. The volumes you can find are as interesting as they are diverse. It's like a great big treasure hunt for literary geeks.

My Adventure: _____

_____

_____

Date: _____

9. Take a CPR or first aid class.

Libraries are not just a source for books and periodicals, they're an integral part of the community. As such, they often offer classes and programs designed to help the neighborhoods they serve. If you've ever wanted to learn CPR or basic first aid – check out the library first. ("Check out" the library...see what I did there?)

My Adventure: _____

_____

_____

Date: _____

10. Attend a lunch & learn program.

I once worked in a downtown setting, and at the time the downtown area was a place people went to work, not live. So the downtown library branch came up with a creative way to entice people to use its services. They offered a "lunch & learn" program. Once a week they brought in a speaker, and people who worked downtown could bring their bagged lunch to the library and enjoy a fascinating hour learning about various topics.

My Adventure: _____

_____

_____

Date: _____

11. Get a little peace and quiet.

One of the best kept secrets of the library is its ability to function as a satellite office. Now, I'm not suggesting you have the address changed on your business cards. But if you ever need a change of place to read or work and use free wifi (or escape the incessant sound of construction from the remodeling project next door), head to the library.

My Adventure: _____

_____

_____

Date: _____

12. Just go!

Usage and community value are factors that can affect a library's budget when local government leaders prepare their budget each year – so use them or lose them! In my opinion, libraries are one of the must under-appreciated and under-utilized resources we have. Knowledge is power, and there is limitless knowledge available at our fingertips (for free!) at your local library. So go! Don't let this indispensable resource disappear for lack of use. Go!

My Adventure: _____

_____

_____

Date: _____

Apps

1. Duolingo.

Duolingo is one my favorite apps. It's a great way to learn a language. The app takes you through the language gradually, and reinforces what you've learned along the way so it "sticks." And the best part – it's FREE!

My Adventure: _____

_____

_____

Date: _____

2. Khan Academy.

Khan Academy was developed by an educator who wanted to provide free online educational support for students. You can learn about almost any subject you'd like – and it's free.

My Adventure: _____

_____

_____

Date: _____

3. PhotoMath.

For me, sometimes it's easier to work backwards. And that's what PhotoMath does. Simply point your phone's camera at a math problem, and the app will tell you the solution. And here's the best part – it will also walk you through step-by-step how it reached the solution. Now that's my kind of learning.

My Adventure: _____

_____

_____

Date: _____

4. YouTube.

The question is, what *can't* you learn on YouTube? This is the most popular site for "how-to" everything. From changing your oil, to tap dancing, to playing guitar, to doing your hair – it's all on there.

My Adventure: _____

_____

_____

Date: _____

5. SideChef.

OK, this one's really cool. SideChef is not your usual cooking app. It's designed for all levels of cooks (yes – even the cooking-phobic can succeed with this app), and takes you step-by-step through the recipe. But here's the really cool part. It responds to voice commands, so you don't have to handle your phone with messy foody hands. It also has a built-in timer, so it "cooks" right along with you. And, you can search its database of recipes by what you have on hand. Awesome, huh?

My Adventure: _____

_____

_____

Date: _____

6. SoloLearn.

If you've ever wanted to jump into the hot market of computer programming, this app is for you. SoloLearn teaches you how to code – and it's free! As of this writing, they had over 940 lessons covering all the major coding languages. Who knows – you could become the next internet whiz-kid multi-billionaire. (You're welcome.)

My Adventure: _____

_____

_____

Date: _____

7. Udemy.

This app offers a variety of courses on everything from computer programming to yoga. When you view its course list you'll be overwhelmed by all the choices. A word of warning: Udemy is not the creator of its content, it is a marketplace where other content creators can sell their content. And, just like any marketplace, you have to be aware and educated about what you're buying.

My Adventure: _____

_____

_____

Date: _____

8. DIY Car Maintenance.

If you're not a gear-head, this app may be for you. It's a step-by-step car maintenance app that walks you through all the basics. It covers things like changing a tire, changing the oil, checking the fluids, etc. And once you download the app, you don't have to be online to use it.

My Adventure: _____

_____

_____

Date: _____

9. GradeProof.

On the outside, the GradeProof app appears to be a simple academic app to proof spelling and grammar, and check for plagiarization. But it's more than that. GradeProof can help you become a better writer by suggesting improvements to your writing and to refine your work and make it more eloquent.

My Adventure: _____

_____

_____

Date: _____

10. EdX.

Ever wanted to take a class from Harvard? MIT? The Smithsonian? With EdX you can. EdX offers free online classes on hundreds of subjects from leading universities, museums, and more.

My Adventure: _____

_____

_____

Date: _____

11. HeadSpace.

Learn to lessen stress and worry, and increase peacefulness and happiness by reshaping your brain. Learning how to meditate online in just 10 minutes a day can reap huge rewards in your quality of life.

My Adventure: _____

_____

_____

Date: _____

Community Center

1. Dance classes.

Community center dance classes aren't just for kids anymore. Adults can have as much fun learning a new way to cut a rug. Me? I'm going to take a hula class. I hear it's good exercise to whittle away the waistline.

My Adventure: _____

_____

_____

Date: _____

2. Cooking classes.

My local community center offers all kinds of cooking classes in ethnic foods, cooking with kids, romantic menus, and even classes in the basics. I will gladly pay to use someone else's kitchen and let them do the dishes.

My Adventure: _____

_____

_____

Date: _____

3. Software classes.

A friend of mine is a certified Photoshop whiz, and he shares his skills with the community. The great thing about taking software classes at a community center is that the center already has the software on their system. So if you want to learn a program that's traditionally very expensive (like Photoshop), you don't have to worry about shelling out a bunch of dough to buy the software before you even know how to use it.

My Adventure: _____

_____

_____

Date: _____

4. Gadget classes.

We're not all equally tech savvy. Some people have a more natural inclination towards digital gadgets than others. So if you're the kind who was not born with a smartphone in your hands, perhaps a gadget class is for you. Learn how to outsmart your smartphone, to keep tabs on your tablet, or to navigate your GPS. Sadly, there are still no classes on how to set the clock on your VCR. (What's a VCR?)

My Adventure: _____

_____

_____

Date: _____

5. Swimming lessons.

As a little girl, I took swimming lessons through my community center. They didn't have a pool at the center itself, so they partnered with the local public pool and hired swimming pros to teach classes for all ages. If they only offered a class on how to *not* be terrified to jump off the high dive, that would have been great.

My Adventure: _____

_____

_____

Date: _____

6. Lectures.

Since community centers are focused on the communities they serve, they often host events relevant to the local area. They bring in subject matter experts to speak on topics ranging from conservation and bird watching to crime and politics, and everything in between.

My Adventure: _____

_____

_____

Date: _____

7. Historical events.

Every area has history. It might not be the kind of history to be featured in history textbooks, but it's important to your local area, and fundamental to the formation of your community. And sometimes that's the most interesting of all.

My Adventure: _____

_____

_____

Date: _____

8. Crafts

Community centers are a hub of creativity. Crafters of all ages can have a heyday with all the classes offered. From paper crafts to fabric crafts to woodworking and beyond, get your craft on and join a class.

My Adventure: _____

_____

_____

Date: _____

Art Galleries/Museums

1. Lecture series.

Check out your local museum for learning opportunities. Often, when a new exhibit premiers, museums and art galleries host lecture series for its patrons to learn about the art, artist, and often the culture and history behind the works being exhibited. Even if you're not a fan of the artist, the educational lectures can be very interesting and entertaining.

My Adventure: _____

_____

_____

Date: _____

2. Guest speakers.

Museums often have theaters and event space where non-museum related activities are held. I recently attended a debate between a Christian Theologian and an atheist about the existence of God. While it loosely corresponded to an exhibit, it also held its own as a stand-alone event. Check out your museum's or art gallery's web page for a calendar of upcoming events.

My Adventure: _____

_____

_____

Date: _____

3. Art classes.

What better place to learn than surrounded by the works of masters in an art gallery or museum? Most larger museums offer sketching, painting, and drawing classes for art lovers of all ages and levels.

My Adventure: _____

_____

_____

Date: _____

4. History classes.

History and museums go hand-in-hand. Since most art reflects the social, economic, and political climates of the times during which they're painted, they are a fascinating peek into days gone by. And what better way to learn about centuries past than with visual aids?

My Adventure: _____

_____

_____

Date: _____

5. Flora/fauna classes.

Museums with garden space usually offer architecture and garden tours of their grounds. Additionally, many arboretums consider themselves outdoor museums, housing plant and tree species worthy of a museum exhibit, as well as statue gardens and impressive fountains.

My Adventure: _____

_____

_____

Date: _____

6. Special shows.

Museums aren't limited to oil paintings of yesteryear. There are many museums focusing on specialty subjects. So, go see a concert at the Rock & Roll museum. Or, see an air show at the Planes of Fame museum. Or attend a pow-wow at the Native American museum.

My Adventure: _____

_____

_____

Date: _____

Jennifer Lynn O'Hara

11

TIME SAVING TIP #7

Join forces!

Children are a blessing. We've all heard the mantra. And while that may be true, we cannot ignore the hard truth of having kids. They can suck your time away like no other force on the planet.

Along with being one of the greatest experiences of your life, being a parent can also be the most overwhelming, frustrating, maddening, and tiring job you'll ever have. And let's face it – as much as we love 'em, sometimes we just need a break.

That's where your friends and family network comes in.

Join forces with your fellow parent friends to organize a kind of "child swap" one night a week (or month, or whatever schedule works for you). On the scheduled night, kids gather at a designated house for a 2-3 hour play date. The host parents can organize a movie night, a game night, a craft night – the options are endless. The host house and parents rotate on a schedule, so everyone takes turns being the host and gathering place. While the kids are at their play date, you get a few "extra" hours. The more people participating, the more "extra" time parents get.

Obviously, there are a lot of logistics you'll need to work out. You'll want to get to know the participating families and make sure each environment is safe. If your child has any allergies or other challenges, each host parent should be made aware. But once all the details are sorted, and everyone feels comfortable, this kind of play-date-swap is a win-win for both kids and parents.

If you don't have a network of friends with children, get involved with your local church. There are almost always families with young children at church. Also – check to see if there's a local family co-op in your area. This type of arrangement might already exist near you, just waiting for you to join in.

12

TIME SAVING TIP #8

Learn to say no or let it go!

Society tells us that good citizens are also people-pleasers. And an even greater value is placed on that virtue if you happen to be female. This societal norm is sometimes the very thing that keeps us from doing everything we're meant to do. We spend so much time worrying about disappointing others, or wanting to look good to others, that we say yes to things we shouldn't. Or, and probably more accurately, we're afraid to say no to the things we should for fear of looking bad or selfish. This often results in us spending our most precious resource – time – on non-beneficial tasks. And that forces us to sacrifice what may bring the most value to our own lives.

Now, I'm not saying to go out there and mow down people as if they are merely obstacles to be obliterated, just because they ask us to do something. After all, I have an entire chapter in this book that extols the merits of volunteering and giving back. Studies show that volunteering, helping others, and giving of ourselves are the things that also lead to the most happiness and greatest sense of fulfillment.

So, how do I reconcile these two? How can I suggest we say "no" more often, and also say "yes" more often? Simple. By ensuring that the things we say "yes" to are worthy of the time-price we will pay.

Do you ever notice that you're the only one who makes cookies/cupcakes for the class? Or the only one who organizes the party? Do you always load the dishwasher or do the laundry because you know if anyone else does it it won't be done the "right" way? Do you find that there's someone who's always the delegator while you're always the do-er? Look at these patterns, and have an honest discussion with yourself about where you fall in these scenarios. We get so busy putting others' needs before our own, or we're so afraid to say no, that our own lives and those of our families often suffer as a result.

It's time to put an end to that cycle. It's time to say no, or let it go.

So, the next time you're asked for the umpteen-millionth time to be the "go-to" person for something, ask yourself two questions; 1) Am I the only, or most appropriate, person who can complete this task? And, 2) is the time-price I'll pay for it worth the exchange?

If the answer to either of these questions is "no," then

you should question whether you really need to take on the task.

But before you get all militant in your "nos," remember there are ways to soften the "no" delivery. Instead of agreeing to spend several hours making 64 cupcakes from scratch, suggest picking up pre-made cupcakes from the store. Instead of agreeing to spend an entire week decorating the whole church by yourself, offer to lead a group of volunteers to spend two days doing it (but be sure to include the caveat that if no one volunteers, it won't get done). Instead of holding on to rigid rules about how the dishwasher should be loaded, learn to appreciate a haphazardly loaded dishwasher and be thankful that it's being done by someone other than you for a change.

Once you get the hang of it, you'll find there's great freedom in saying no and letting go. And, surprise, you may find that people will respect you more, not less, if you do.

Jennifer Lynn O'Hara

13

BECOME

New Year's Resolutions are full of good intentions. Most involve some kind of "becoming" goal, such as "I want to be healthier/wealthier/wiser," etc. But the majority of those well-intentioned self-promises never make it to February. Don't give up on those lofty goals. Make a plan to create extra time each week and turn those midnight promises into daytime realities.

☐

Fit

1. Hit the gym.

This one is so obvious, I feel like I'm cheating by including it. But I'll mention it anyway. There are so many inexpensive gyms available today. Do your research and find one that fits your budget. My gym only costs me $20/month, and I can bring a friend anytime I like. What's more motivating than that?

My Adventure: _____

_____

_____

Date: _____

2. Workout at home.

If a gym membership, even a cheap one, is out of your budget, work out at home with a DVD. Thrift stores are loaded with workout DVDs (a graveyard of New Year's Eve resolutions, I suspect). So do yourself a favor and pick up a couple. Cheap DVDs and some willpower are all you need to take your first step toward good health.

My Adventure: _____

_____

_____

Date: _____

3. Join an online fitness service.

There are countless online fitness services available to tech-centric health enthusiasts. Most will have pre-planned workouts, and they automatically switch up your routine so you (and your muscles) don't get bored with the same ol' same ol'. Some services charge a monthly fee, but many are free. (Bonus if it has a support group to commiserate with your aches and pains.)

My Adventure: _____

_____

_____

Date: _____

4. Take a walk.

If you don't want to spend a penny getting healthy, you're in luck! Your next workout is just a step out your front door. Take a walk around your neighborhood. Lengthen the walk a little each day, and before you know it, you'll be on your way to a healthier you.

My Adventure: _____

_____

_____

Date: _____

5. Ride a bike.

As a kid I loved to ride my bike. The sheer joy and freedom of having the wheels under me and the wind in my face was magic. But something happens when we grow up, and that simple joy starts to vanish from memory. Between work and adult responsibilities, riding just for fun became a luxury. So reclaim that youthful exuberance, get on your bike, and ride like the wind!

My Adventure: _____

_____

_____

Date: _____

6. Go jogging.

This is a hard one for me to recommend because I generally don't run unless there's a T-Rex or bee chasing me. But then my friend introduced me to Couch to 5k. This miraculous little app does just what it implies. It takes you from the couch to running a 5K. It starts very gradually – jog 60 seconds, walk 60 seconds, etc –then works up to jogging a full 5K. I no longer hate jogging. I don't love it, but not hating is a huge step forward for me. So give it a try – it's free.

My Adventure: _____

_____

_____

Date: _____

7. Visit the roller/ice skating ring.

This is another joy from childhood that seems to get pushed aside once we reluctantly cross over into the humdrum world of adulting. But don't let it happen! Get out those skates and glide your way to fitness. The balance, core strength, and muscle power required will get you in shape in no time. And if you laugh as much as I do while skating, you'll get a good ab workout, too.

My Adventure: _____

_____

_____

Date: _____

8. Go horseback riding.

How often do you see a fat cowboy? Not often. You know why? Because horseback riding burns a LOT of calories! It doesn't seem like it would, after all, the horse is doing the work. But take a look at calorie-counting websites and you'll see horseback riding is actually great exercise. And it's a heck of a lot of fun, too. If you don't have a horse, or friends with horses, find a stable that rents by the hour. It's a bit pricey but worth every penny.

My Adventure: _____

_____

_____

Date: _____

9. Buy a fitness tracker.

Whether you use a Fitbit, Garmin, or just an app on your phone, studies have shown that using some sort of fitness tracker helps people be more aware of their activity levels (or lack thereof), and stay accountable to exercise goals. Or, for more interactive fun, challenge your friends to a little healthy competition.

My Adventure: _____

_____

_____

Date: _____

10. Do a half marathon.

Challenge yourself to sign up for a ½ (or full) marathon, then train accordingly. Start early and train smartly. There are countless apps out there to help get you in shape. If you're new to running, start with the Couch to 5K app. Then transition to a marathon training app or calendar plan. You'll have race medals hanging on your brag wall in no time.

My Adventure: _____

_____

_____

Date: _____

11. Try rock climbing.

Rock climbing is a "thing" now. All the cool kids are doing it. In fact, many activity centers and fitness clubs have installed rock climbing walls as part of their facilities' offerings, and there are entire companies that do nothing but offer indoor thrill/skill sports like rock climbing. You don't have to drive to Yosemite and scale El Capitan. Find a small wall to summit in your own town.

My Adventure: _____

_____

_____

Date: _____

12. Do Yoga or Tai Chi.

Don't let the slow pace fool you; yoga can kick you in the butt. I think there may be a yoga move where you actually kick yourself there. (Just kidding. I think.) Yoga and tai chi both focus on balance and control. Yoga has varying degrees of difficulty from "This is nice" to "Oh my gosh I'm going to die!" Choose the one that's best for you, then downward dog your way to better health.

My Adventure: _____

_____

_____

Date: _____

13. Learn martial arts or other self-defense.

Martial arts and self-defense classes have the dual benefit of improving health and teaching a valuable skill. For your own comfort level, try out different studios (or dojos) to find one that fits you best. Most offer classes geared toward women, teens, or kids, and focus on specifics such as practical self-defense.

My Adventure: _____

_____

_____

Date: _____

14. Gamify your workout.

Use WiiFit or a similar video game fitness platform to combine your video game habit with your workout routine. Most video game fitness platforms will let you work out with friends in a virtual environment. It's a great way to combine fitness, fun, and far-away friends.

My Adventure: _____

_____

_____

Date: _____

Creative

1. Write.

Write a short story. We've all had ideas that have make us think, "That would make a great story." Well, now's your chance. Jot down those ideas, then use your four extra hours to turn them into a short story. Expand your story into a novel if it lends itself to it. Then use a self-publishing platform to publish your work.

My Adventure: _____

_____

_____

Date: _____

2. Compose.

Have you ever woken up in the middle of the night with your own made-up song stuck in your head? If that happens, use the record feature on your phone to capture the melody before it evaporates like a dream. Then, when you're awake, turn your nocturnal composing into a song. Or, if poetry is your thing, jot down song ideas, then turn them into song lyrics.

My Adventure: _____

_____

_____

Date: _____

3. Paint.

Channel your inner Bob Ross and learn to paint. Or if you're already a master, break out those canvases and start layering color. Your next masterpiece is only a few brushstrokes away. If you're new to painting, take a class or buy an instructional DVD to walk you through the basics. It really is easier than you think. And if you still need more convincing, sign up for one of those "sip-and-paint" nights where you learn step-by-step how to paint an image, and you walk away with a finished piece.

My Adventure: _____

_____

_____

Date: _____

4. Craft.

Whether your preferred craft is scrapbooking, quilting, decoupage, or clay, four extra hours is plenty of time to indulge in a little recreational crafting. Most people I know have a craft room, cabinet, or shelf. It's time to blow the dust off of those craft supplies and put them to use.

My Adventure: _____

_____

_____

Date: _____

5. Make homemade gifts.

When I say "homemade gifts," I don't mean picture frames made of macaroni and gold spray paint. (Unless you're four.) I mean gifts your friends and family will love. If you're a cooking wiz, make a batch of artisan jams. If your talents lie with the sewing machine, make quilts. If you paint, create masterpieces. Homemade gifts are often cheaper, and almost always more appreciated, than a store-bought afterthought.

My Adventure: _____

_____

_____

Date: _____

6. Write letters.

I mean letters – not emails or texts – actual letters with pen, paper, envelopes, and stamps. Letter writing is becoming a lost art, so brighten someone's day and put pen to paper to let them know you're thinking about them. (OK, I'll give you a break here. A well-chosen greeting card with a note inside is fine in a pinch.)

My Adventure: _____

_____

_____

Date: _____

7. Practice an instrument.

The key to getting good at anything is practicing. As a musician myself, I know how un-fun practicing can be. But if music is important to you, you will enjoy it all the more if you have some level of proficiency. And there's no other way to gain proficiency than to practice. So bite the bullet and tune up that instrument. You'll thank me later.

My Adventure: _____

_____

_____

Date: _____

Fashion/Beauty

1. Get a make-over.

When I graduated from school in 19*mumblemumble* the make-up trends were very specific. With each passing season, trends change. But our busy lives usually prevent us from studying the latest issues of *Cosmo* or *Vogue* to learn what's new and trendy. So, we tend to get stuck in those old-school make-up habits...blue eyeshadow and all. Break out of your make-up rut and get a make-over at a department store beauty counter. The make-overs are usually free, but it's customary to buy an item and/or tip the person doing the make-over.

My Adventure: _____

_____

_____

Date: _____

2. Get your hair done.

Take an hour or two to treat yourself. Go to a blow-dry bar and get a professional style. Or, go big and get a cut or color. You'll feel like a new person. And you know what? You deserve it!

My Adventure: _____

_____

_____

Date: _____

3. Learn a new hair style.

We can't afford to go to the stylist every day to get our hair done, and the basic ponytail gets pretty boring day-in, day-out. So take a few minutes to learn how to do a new do. YouTube is a great source for this. There are countless video tutorials on how to do virtually any style you want. Like most things, it takes practice. But you'll be a hair maestro in no time.

My Adventure: _____

_____

_____

Date: _____

4. Attend a beauty party.

The latest trend in in-home product parties is the beauty party. They're not the Avon parties of the 1960s (although those are still around, too). Instead, they're updated with the latest products and gadgets. You can even go to a Botox party! (Just make sure there's a certified health professional administering the procedure.)

My Adventure: _____

_____

_____

Date: _____

5. Get a facial.

Day spas offer coupons on discount websites all the time. Take advantage of a great deal and treat yourself to a facial. Facials are relaxing and good for the skin. Just make sure you don't have any plans the week after your first one, just in case you get any unexpected breakouts.

My Adventure: _____

_____

_____

Date: _____

6. Get an old-fashioned shave.

OK – this section started sounding a little too girl-centric, so this one's for the dudes. Treat yourself to an old-fashioned shave. You know – the kind where you go to a barber shop, lean back in a chair, and swap stories with the barber while he uses a straight edge razor to rid your face of stubble. Finish with a hot towel wrap. Cary Grant would settle for nothing less.

My Adventure: _____

_____

_____

Date: _____

7. Read a fashion magazine.

If it's been a while since you've had a wardrobe update, take a few minutes to read a fashion magazine or two before shopping. You'll see what is trendy and what is still classic. From there you can evaluate your wardrobe and determine what pieces can be worked into an updated closet.

My Adventure: _____

_____

_____

Date: _____

8. Try on clothes at the mall.

Have you recently lost or gained weight? Or just haven't bought new clothes in a long time and have no idea how the new trends look on you? Take a trip to the mall for reconnaissance purposes only. Walk around, look at displays, and choose a whole bunch of things at different stores to try on. Don't get discouraged – you're not there to buy. Just try stuff on and see what looks good. Then when you're ready to buy, you'll know where to focus.

My Adventure: _____

_____

_____

Date: _____

9. Take a bubble bath.

The romanticized idea of a candlelit bubble bath has endured through the decades for a reason. For many, it is the ultimate luxury – all that's missing is the cabana boy peeling grapes. Even without a handsome man doting on your every whim, a bubble bath can still be your own personal luxury. Take a few minutes, light some candles, pour a glass of wine, and indulge in bubbly goodness.

My Adventure: _____

_____

_____

Date: _____

10. Get a manicure and/or pedicure.

This one isn't just for the girls. Guys, I'm talking to you, too! Foot hygiene is very important, and can be a dating deal-breaker. So do yourself (and your partner) a favor and take care of your tootsies. The best thing about getting a mani/pedi is sitting in the comfy chair and not doing a thing while trained professionals clean up those hard-working hands and feet. Since most techs also give hand/feet massages as part of the normal service, it's a two-for-one package; nice nails and a massage. Ahhhh...

My Adventure: _____

_____

_____

Date: _____

11. Host a clothes swap.

Organize a clothing/shoe swap with your friends. Remember those clothing items you loved in the store, but when you got them home you realized they just didn't look right with the shoes? Everyone has those items in their closet. Have your friends bring their in-style but seldom worn clothes to your house. Open a bottle of wine, serve some snacks, and have fun trying on and swapping outfits.

My Adventure: _____

_____

_____

Date: _____

Health

1. Essential oils.

The use of essential oils to improve health is a centuries-old tradition that is seeing a rebirth. There are hundreds and thousands of stories of people whose health benefited from the use of essential oils. So, do a little research and see what they can do for you.

My Adventure: _____
_____
_____

Date: _____

2. Herbs.

Herbs are the first cousins of essential oils. In fact, many essential oils come from herbs. Herbs have been used for centuries in Chinese medicine. Is it a coincidence that those who eat a traditional Chinese diet and take herbal medicines have some of the lowest rates of chronic diseases? The research is still ongoing, but most experts agree that adding healing herbs to your diet adds a boost to overall health.

My Adventure: _____
_____
_____

Date: _____

3. Foods.

It's no secret that processed foods and fast foods are not healthy options. But fresh, whole foods don't have a long shelf life, and cooking can be a time-consuming hassle. So what should we do? Take your four extra hours and do a little research. Find good, wholesome recipes that can be made in 15-30 minutes (or via low-maintenance methods, such as a slow cooker), and practice your healthy cooking techniques. I guarantee there are a bunch of delicious whole-food recipes that take less time to prepare than it takes to go through a drive-thru.

My Adventure: _____

_____

_____

Date: _____

4. Massage.

Massages don't just feel good, they're also therapeutic. Massages can release toxins that have built up in muscle tissue. They can also relax muscles that are causing spinal misalignment and other joint strain. Oh, yeah – and they feel good, too.

My Adventure: _____

_____

_____

Date: _____

5. Acupuncture.

Acupuncture is another ancient procedures that has proven successful in other cultures, but remains an outlier in the U.S. Many people swear by it, and studies report numerous examples of people helped by acupuncture. I'm told that even the needle-phobic among us need not fear, because the needles are so small they are barely felt.

My Adventure: _____

_____

_____

Date: _____

6. Acupressure and reflexology.

Acupressure and reflexology are both touch therapies. Although they work under different principals, they are often used together. In an over-simplified explanation, acupressure focuses on over 800 pressure points in the body, whereas reflexology focuses on body maps on the hands and feet. The idea is that every area of the body is connected to other areas of the body, and healing can be encouraged by stimulating specific pressure points.

My Adventure: _____

_____

_____

Date: _____

7. Go to bed early/sleep in.

Getting a good night's sleep is one of the best things we can do for our health. Unfortunately, most of us find ourselves lacking the time to do the stuff we need to get done. So use your four extra hours to finish those tasks, and then do yourself a favor and get some sleep.

My Adventure: _____

_____

_____

Date: _____

8. Take a nap.

Naps don't take the place of a good night's sleep, but there are still tremendous health benefits to napping. Our brains get a chance to rest, our bodies feel restored, and our moods are often lifted after taking a nap. But don't get carried away. While a three-hour marathon nap might seem like a good idea, studies have shown that a 20-30 minute power nap is all we need to get the boost we seek.

My Adventure: _____

_____

_____

Date: _____

9. Track your nutrition.

Download and use an app like MyFitnessPal or LoseIt! to track your calories, nutritional intake, and exercise. It's a bit overwhelming at first to remember to track every single thing you eat. But if you are diligent, what you get at the end of the day is an accurate picture of what you're putting into your body. You might be shocked at how good or bad your diet really is. And when it comes to improving your health, knowledge is power. So use the knowledge to elevate your health and fitness level.

My Adventure: _____

_____

_____

Date: _____

10. Plant plants.

We should all remember the days of grade school chemistry when we learned that, through the process of photosynthesis, plants clean the air by taking in carbon dioxide and releasing oxygen. Some plants are better oxygen producers than others. So, clean your indoor air by finding and placing clean air plants around your home.

My Adventure: _____

_____

_____

Date: _____

11. Mental break.

Take a camping/hiking hammock to your local beach or park, find two accommodating trees, and enjoy a little mental health break. Bring a book to read, or don't. It's your call. The main goal is to let your brain escape the pressure and stress of everyday life by taking a mini mental vacation.

My Adventure: _____

_____

_____

Date: _____

Financial

1. Join an investment club.

Investing can be a scary thing – especially if you are not a financial whiz kid. But there's an easy and non-intimidating way to get started. Investment clubs are a way to dip your toe into investing with the help and non-judgmental support of friends. The best part about investing with a group is that you can all celebrate together, commiserate together, and maybe have a margarita or two along the way.

My Adventure: _____

_____

_____

Date: _____

2. Turn your craft DIY into an online store.

Between Etsy, Ebay, and all the other online selling sites, the outlets for your creativity are numerous. Take a few minutes of your four extra hours and figure out which of your creative talents would sell the best (and for the most), then get on to production.

My Adventure: _____

_____

_____

Date: _____

3. Buy at thrift, sell on eBay.

If you are addicted to thrift shopping, perhaps a buy/sell business is for you. Thrift stores and yard sales are often full of name brand merchandise that does very well in the resale arena. I rented a booth at an antique mall and re-sold the treasures I'd pick up for pennies at the local thrift stores. When curated with other items in a professional display, thrift store finds become valued collectibles. I only averaged $100-$200 profit a month, but it justified my thrifting habit and that was enough for me.

My Adventure: _____

_____

_____

Date: _____

4. Have a yard sale.

Clean out your clutter and make extra cash by having a yard sale. Sure it's a whole lotta work to go through your stuff, organize it, tag it, put up yard sale signs, and man your sale all day in the heat of summer, but think of what you get in return. You get the double-whammy benefit of a less-cluttered house and a thicker wallet.

My Adventure: _____

_____

_____

Date: _____

5. Use an financial tracking app.

A good way to manage spending is to use a budgeting app like Mint, Shoeboxed, or other finance tracker. These apps connect with your cards and track your spending. It sorts spending into categories and lets you see where you can improve your spending/saving behaviors. But beware – you may learn that your $40/month Starbucks habit is really a $200/month habit, and that is a pretty tough pill to swallow. Not that I'm speaking from experience here. This is all just hypothetical. Really, it is.

My Adventure: _____

_____

_____

Date: _____

6. Create a budget.

It might take some time to set it up, and perhaps 30 minutes a week to do a financial check-in, but the process of creating a budget is the first step to financial freedom. The trick is to make a plan and stick to it. Both halves of this financial equation are necessary to make progress.

My Adventure: _____

_____

_____

Date: _____

7. Read a book.

There are new books and magazines on money management on the market every day. Find one and read it (bonus points if you check it out from the library). Investing is a scary thing for many of us, and we're often afraid of looking stupid, so we don't ask for help. Educate yourself in the privacy of your own home by reading up on the subject before talking to fellow investors or money management professionals.

My Adventure: _____

_____

_____

Date: _____

8. Use an investment app.

Invest without having to think about it by using an app like Acorns. This clever little app ties to your spending cards, and then rounds up your purchases to the next whole dollar. All that spare change is then invested every month into the funds you choose. It's amazing how all those pennies add up to some nice investments.

My Adventure: _____

_____

_____

Date: _____

9. Pay off your debt.

Use your phone to help pay down debt. Much like the Acorns app, the Qoins app rounds up your purchases and sets aside that money. Once a month it redistributes all those accumulated funds to the credit card of your choice. Once that card is paid off, switch the Qoins app to the next card on your pay-off list.

My Adventure: _____

_____

_____

Date: _____

Jennifer Lynn O'Hara

14

TIME SAVING TIP #9

Exercise in the morning!

I used to hate working out in the morning. Wait. Scratch that. I use to hate working out. Period. Especially running. I abhor running.

But then a friend convinced me to use the Couch to 5K app to get ready to do a big 5K race in our town. OK, fine, whatever. In the name of friendship I'll do it. And I promise I'll hate very single second.

And you know what happened? I was right. I hated every single second of running.

But then an amazing thing happened. I noticed when I started my day with a 2 or 3 mile run (oh, heck – let's call it what it is – a jog), I got SO much accomplished the rest of the day. I expected to go home and be a completely exhausted shell of a human after my run/jog. But the opposite happened. I felt invincible. I felt like I could conquer the world. I had energy and motivation I didn't know what to do with. I tackled tasks like a champ. I got two days' worth of work done in a single day. Now that's some serious time saving!!! It's made me love running!

OK – let's not get too carried away. I still hate running. But I love it when I stop. And I've learned that if I invest a little time in the morning to exercise, I earn that time back 10-fold in productivity the rest of the day.

And in case you're not convinced, here are some more fun facts. There have been extensive studies on the effects of exercising on the mind and body. Exercising in the morning improves focus and mental ability. Exercise has a greater impact than caffeine. And here's my favorite: Exercise boosts metabolism and burns calories at a faster pace up to 14 hours after working out – even while just sitting at a desk.

15

TIME SAVING TIP #10

Make a list, keep a calendar, and set daily goals!

Use a calendar to keep track of your big to-do items so you know how much time you have to work on them. Then add milestone markers to hit along the way to keep you on track. Finally, make a detailed list each day and prioritize it in order of importance. Focus on that list and work on it in priority order without jumping around or giving in to the urge to check your social media accounts.

A lot of time is wasted flitting from task to task. It's easy to get distracted, so put away all those things that tug at your attention. The brain can only hold about seven pieces of information at a time. If you jump around to multiple projects, you will have to re-enter the information that has been bumped out of your brain. The act of rebooting your thought process takes time, which ultimately increases the time it takes to complete a project. Sure it may only take a few seconds to refocus your thoughts – but those seconds add up quickly.

If you're an app person, use an app like Evernote, where you can create lists and set reminders. Whatever you don't check off your list today should be rolled over to tomorrow's list.

To avoid getting sucked into the black hole of distractions, set blocks of time to do specific tasks – and purposefully eliminate all possible distractions during those time blocks. Put them on your calendaring or list app, and treat them like appointments with yourself. Focus only on the task at hand during that time. You'll find you get significantly more done by dedicating a block of time to a single task than by bouncing from task to task.

16

HELP

There is an old Chinese proverb that says, in part, "If you want happiness for an hour, take a nap. If you want happiness for a lifetime, help somebody." Science has also proven this. Numerous academic studies and surveys show that the happiest people are those who are involved in helping others. So make an investment in your own happiness by investing your four extra hours helping others.

☐

Volunteer

1. Sign up with a volunteer match organization.

If you are unsure of where to begin your volunteer work, there are many volunteer match organizations that act as clearing houses for volunteer events. Many small groups and non-profit organizations don't have the visibility of the nationally known organizations, so they add their events to these sites, who then match the volunteer event with people who have expressed interest in that field.

My Adventure: _____
_____
_____

Date: _____

2. Join forces with charitable organizations.

There are so many charitable organizations it would take a volume of books to list them all. Volunteers of America, Meals on Wheels, Project Angel Food, soup kitchens, Habitat for Humanity, Arbor Day Foundation, animal shelters, etc., etc., etc. Find one that fits your volunteer style and the programs you're passionate about, and give them a bit of your four extra hours.

My Adventure: _____
_____
_____

Date: _____

3. Support your political beliefs.

Get involved in the decisions that affect your life by volunteering for your political party. Sometimes we feel the need to do more than just cast our vote. Getting involved with your political party's grassroots-level initiatives is a good place to start. Contact your local representative to see how you can help.

My Adventure: _____

_____

_____

Date: _____

4. Make blessing bags.

Create blessing bags for people in need. Each bag should contain basic essentials like lip balm, baby wipes, socks, Band-Aids, & lotion. Leave out those things that contain alcohol (like hand sanitizer) or anything super smelly. Also, you can leave out the soap – most places that have running water also have soap. Go in groups to hand them out or take them to a local shelter to distribute.

My Adventure: _____

_____

_____

Date: _____

5. Get involved with letters/treats for troops.

Contact a troop support organization and write letters to troops. Most people know about sending cards for the holidays, but there are 11 other months in a year. Letters from home, even from a stranger, are appreciated. Or, donate individually-packaged food items to Treats for Troops or Packages for Patriots. Service men and women get fed, but they don't get the "fun" stuff. And when you're a couple thousand miles from home, a pack of Oreos can go a long way to brighten your day.

My Adventure: _____

_____

_____

Date: _____

6. Donate to a local charity.

After you've cleaned out your closets, it's sometimes more beneficial to donate your stuff to a local charity than to have a yard sale. When you donate to a charity, you can take a tax write-off that is often larger than what you'd earn in a yard sale. So figure out what's best for you and let a charity benefit from your clean-out.

My Adventure: _____

_____

_____

Date: _____

7. Go on a charity grocery binge.

Set a spending limit – $20, $40, etc. – and go to your local dollar store for a grocery shopping binge. Focus on healthy foods, but include a couple fun things as well. Then take your bounty to a women's shelter or food pantry.

My Adventure: _____

_____

_____

Date: _____

8. Plant trees.

Earth Day is the most popular day to join a tree planting expedition. But trees are planted and maintained all year 'round. Many groups partner with community and neighborhood beautification organizations to plant trees and other landscaping. So get your hands dirty and plant a tree.

My Adventure: _____

_____

_____

Date: _____

9. Help with a neighborhood fix-it day.

Partner with a neighborhood volunteer organization to participate in a home beautification project for seniors or disabled residents. Projects could range from improving landscaping to painting a house to basic home repairs. You'll make a huge difference in the life of a community member.

My Adventure: _____

_____

_____

Date: _____

10. Read/sing/play/visit at a local senior center.

Reach out to your local senior center and see what kind of volunteer opportunities they have. This is a great way to use your talents to brighten someone else's day. And if you don't have musical ability, offer to read a book to someone with vision problems. Or play a game (maybe even have them teach you how to play one of their favorites). Whatever you do, your time spent with them will be the most appreciated part of your visit.

My Adventure: _____

_____

_____

Date: _____

Community

1. Clean up your community.

Whether you live by the beach, in the mountains, or somewhere in between, groups are always organizing to clean up streets, beaches, trails, and parks. You can even join a group that participates in the "Adopt-a-Highway" program. So get outside, soak up some sun and fresh air, get a little exercise and clean up your community.

My Adventure: _____
_____
_____

Date: _____

2. Participate in community events.

This may not seem like it would fall into the "help" category, but just by attending events you are helping. Without people attending, the event could not be justified and would not happen. Every stage needs an audience, otherwise there's no point. So go and be the audience for your local community events.

My Adventure: _____
_____
_____

Date: _____

3. Beautify a neighborhood.

This activity is a close cousin to the community clean-up project. But instead of cleaning, you're beautifying. Plant flowers in a neighborhood park, weed a community garden, paint joyful murals at a children's hospital, or work with your Department of Public Works or Office of Community Beautification to come up with a project all your own.

My Adventure: _____
_____
_____

Date: _____

4. Work at a public radio and/or television station.

As a kid I remember watching PBS a lot. Big Bird, Bert & Ernie, and all the gang on *Sesame Street* were my friends, and gave me a head start by teaching me words and numbers and how to be a good citizen. PBS also introduced me to the arts, which would became my life. Many of you have similar stories, and owe PBS a debt of gratitude. So give back by volunteering to answer phones at pledge drives. Or stuff envelopes for a big mailing. Or any of the other myriad tasks they need done.

My Adventure: _____
_____
_____

Date: _____

5. Volunteer or donate to a local animal shelter.

Animals are my soft spot. I would adopt them all if I could. But since I can't, I satisfy that need to help by volunteering at a local shelter. My favorites are the cat shelters that have volunteers play with, cuddle, and socialize the cats that are waiting to be adopted. If you'd prefer to donate, shelters have a list of items they always need, like food, blankets, and toys. Check your local shelter to learn ways you can help pets in need.

My Adventure: _____

_____

_____

Date: _____

6. Join local conservancy groups.

If outdoor volunteering is more your style, there are a host of options for you. Join the Nature Conservancy to help protect land. Join the Audubon Society and become one of their citizen scientists. Help the World Wildlife Fund save species from extinction. Help maintain trails by joining the Pacific Crest or Appalachian Trail conservancies. Or, reach out to one of the numerous other outdoor volunteer groups in your region.

My Adventure: _____

_____

_____

Date: _____

7. Join local arts leagues.

Arts organizations are usually powered by an army of volunteers. As such, they are always in need of people willing to share their time and talents. So if you enjoy the theater, ballet, symphony, opera, or other form of performing/fine art, consider helping your favorite arts organization by becoming a volunteer.

My Adventure: _____

_____

_____

Date: _____

8. Be true to your school.

Work with your alma mater's booster club to help with fundraising. Volunteer to sew costumes or build the set for the local high school drama production. Or, contact your local school board or Department of Education to become involved with more general initiatives.

My Adventure: _____

_____

_____

Date: _____

9. Help your community theater.

Community theaters always need help, and it's usually a heck of a lot of fun to get involved. You can volunteer to usher or house manage, sew costumes or build sets, answer phones or stuff envelopes, or even perform on the stage. Whatever your talents, you can find an outlet for them through your community theater.

My Adventure: _____

_____

_____

Date: _____

Library

1. Read for kids.

Do you remember when you were a kid and how much you looked forward to story time? It was my favorite time of day. And sometimes the promise of a bedtime story was the only thing that convinced me to go to bed. There is something special about having a story read to you. Most libraries have story time for children every week. Share your love of books by volunteering to be a reader at your local library.

My Adventure: _____

_____

_____

Date: _____

2. Organize a book drive at your church or school.

Libraries accept book donations. Their librarian reviews each donated book to determine if it is needed in their collection. If it is, it goes on the shelf. If not, it goes into the library's book sale, and the profits benefit the library. Either way it's a win-win.

My Adventure: _____

_____

_____

Date: _____

3. Go yardsaling for libraries.

Visit yard sales and buy DVDs and good-quality books, then donate them to the library. Check with your branch to see if they need a specific type or genre. If they can't use them, they will include them in their book sales, and the profits will go back to the library.

My Adventure: _____

_____

_____

Date: _____

4. Join library bike rides or other community events.

Many libraries have community outreach events, like bike rides and picnics. Check your library's website for upcoming events and get involved. Of course, participation is fun and a well-attended event is a big boon for the library. But you might also call and see if they need any help organizing the event.

My Adventure: _____

_____

_____

Date: _____

5. Help with membership drives.

Some libraries have community advocates who attend fairs, events, and community programs to educate people about the services offered through the library and to boost membership numbers. This is a great way to help your library, but also a wonderful way to meet people in your community.

My Adventure: _____

_____

_____

Date: _____

6. Become a docent.

Aside from the books they lend, libraries can be interesting in-and-of themselves. Many libraries are housed in historic buildings and have art and architecture with a fascinating history all its own. These libraries often offer docent-led tours to tell the building's history and answer questions about the art and architecture. Becoming a docent requires training – but you can use your four extra hours for that, too.

My Adventure: _____

_____

_____

Date: _____

7. Assist with adult literacy programs.

You don't have to be a teacher to assist adult learners. Libraries have literacy programs to help adult learners of all levels. Volunteers are screened and interviewed, and then trained. Then they are assigned an adult learner student, and spend an hour or two each week tutoring them. Subjects range from reading and writing to math and English-speaking skills. What a rewarding experience to be a part of someone else's self-improvement journey!

My Adventure: _____

_____

_____

Date: _____

8. Work as an inventory aide.

If working with the public is not your thing, consider volunteering as a library inventory aid. Hundreds of books are returned each week, and library staff needs help restocking and reorganizing shelves. If you're the kind of person who alphabetizes your DVDs and organizes your closet by color, this might be the job for you. There is nothing quite so rewarding as seeing a neat and tidy shelf of books alphabetized by authors' last name.

My Adventure: _____

_____

_____

Date: _____

9. Become a homework assistant.

OK, I'm not ashamed to admit that this one might be tricky. Teaching styles change frequently, and the classrooms of today are not the classrooms I remember. But if education is your forte, volunteer to be a homework assistant to help kids with their school work. Sure, you might need to brush up on your quadratic equation skills, but isn't it worth it to help a kid do better in school?

My Adventure: _____

_____

_____

Date: _____

10. Share your tech/media skills.

Libraries are usually looking for tech-savvy people to lead basic tech classes. This is the perfect opportunity to let your geek flag fly proudly, and for a good cause. Volunteer to share your passion for all things tech with learners as geeky as you. (And, as a fellow geek, I use that term in the most loving way possible.)

My Adventure: _____

_____

_____

Date: _____

11. Become a program aid.

Those classes and programs don't set themselves up. It takes a small army of helpers to set up for classes, organize materials, assist people, and do all the other odd jobs that make library programs run smoothly. So use your four extra hours to be the hero behind the scenes. They couldn't do it without you.

My Adventure: _____

_____

_____

Date: _____

Church

1. Usher.

Ushers help make sure the church is ready for its guests, pass out programs, and help people find seats. Ushers may also help with collecting the offering or distributing communion. Many churches rotate ushers, so you don't have to worry about over-committing yourself. But even if you do it every week; it only takes a few minutes, and it's a great way to support your church family.

My Adventure: _____

_____

_____

Date: _____

2. Be a greeter.

If you are the outgoing type who always has a smile on your face, this might be the perfect role for you. Greeters are just that – the friendly face who greets visitors at the door. They make people feel welcome, answer questions, and assist first-time visitors. Some greeters also man the donut and coffee tables after service, if your church does that sort of thing.

My Adventure: _____

_____

_____

Date: _____

3. Provide treats for after service.

Many churches offer after-service treats. Some have full-on coffee bars. Whatever your church does, offer to be a part of the food ministry. Bring donuts for after service (hint: you can buy an extra one and eat it on the way to church), or volunteer to serve coffee. Many say that food is the way to a person's soul – and what better way to feed the soul and spirit than combining food and church?

My Adventure: _____

_____

_____

Date: _____

4. Raise funds for missionaries.

Every church has some involvement in missions. Some have their own missionaries in the field. Some adopt a missionary, while others partner with organizations to support ongoing initiatives. All of these require money to operate, and sometimes tithing and donations aren't enough. Speak with church leadership about ways to support your church's missionary endeavors.

My Adventure: _____

_____

_____

Date: _____

5. Teach Sunday school.

You don't have to be a biblical scholar to teach Sunday School. Most churches have a children's ministry director who oversees lesson preparation. Of course, a working knowledge of the Bible is beneficial, but you're not all on your own. Teaching Sunday school can be a rewarding and fun experience, and well worth your extra time.

My Adventure: _____

_____

_____

Date: _____

6. Help with vacation bible school.

Vacation bible school often involves a lot of planning and preparation. Most have themes, decorations, and advertising that need to be done before it begins. Once school starts, there is teaching, plus games, activities, and food. All of this requires volunteers to make it happen. VBS usually only lasts a week or two, so it's an easy commitment that delivers a big impact.

My Adventure: _____

_____

_____

Date: _____

7. "Adopt" a college kid.

Sure, college kids often get care packages from their parents or relatives. But think of how much fun it would be to get a surprise package from a member of their church family. Packages could include the usual stuff college kids survive on (i.e., junk food), but also include more practical items: quarters for laundry, hand sanitizer, toothpaste, etc. Feeling the love from home is a huge blessing to kids flying solo for the first time.

My Adventure: _____

_____

_____

Date: _____

8. Sing in the choir

Maybe you won't be the next Grammy winner, but you can lend your vocal talents to the choir. Choir members rarely sing solos, so you can help round out the sound without having to perform vocal gymnastics. And if you really, truly, can't carry a tune, offer to help in other ways: organize the music library, care for choir robes, set up chairs, etc.

My Adventure: _____

_____

_____

Date: _____

9. Help with the praise team

Many churches today have praise bands leading worship. If your church is one of these, there's plenty to do to assist. If you're musically or vocally inclined, speak to the worship leader to see if you can lend your talents. If you're technically inclined, there are audio and video duties. Often, tech helpers don't need experience – they will train you. Or, you can help with set-up and tear down of equipment.

My Adventure: _____

_____

_____

Date: _____

10. Fresh flowers

Offer to bring in or arrange fresh flowers each week for the entryway or the sanctuary. Many flower shops donate flowers to churches. Or, if your flower garden is abundant, make your own arrangements.

My Adventure: _____

_____

_____

Date: _____

11. Ask your church's leadership how you can help.

Many departments in your church thrive on volunteer input. Ask your Children's Ministry Director how you can help with their job. Ask your Office Administrator if he/she could use a little extra help. Or, offer to lend a hand in the kitchen. There is a volunteer position for every skill set.

My Adventure: _____

_____

_____

Date: _____

Friends/Family

1. Help your mother.

As kids, "help your mother" were the last words you wanted to hear on a weekend that was meant for play. But as an adult, you understand the importance, and the – dare I say it – fun, of helping your parents. As adults, we connect with our parents in ways we weren't capable of as children. So if you're lucky enough to have your parents still with you, share some time with them this weekend.

My Adventure: _____
_____
_____

Date: _____

2. Help your sibling.

Growing up, it felt like my sister and I fought all the time. Constantly. Non-stop. Aye, aye, aye…my poor mother. Today, she is one of my best friends and I cherish our time together. Sure, shopping and lunch are fun, but I have more fun helping her with a chore. It doesn't matter what we do, laughter is guaranteed. So help your sibling turn the mundane into fun and offer to lend a hand.

My Adventure: _____
_____
_____

Date: _____

3. Babysit.

Our siblings/cousins/friends who have children often lack the resources to pay for a babysitter AND a night out. So give your sibling/cousin/friend the gift of a kid-free date night by offering to babysit for free. Chances are they'll return the favor.

My Adventure: _____

_____

_____

Date: _____

4. Help your grandparents.

I wish I had lived closer to my grandparents as an adult. As a kid, I loved going to Grandma and Grandpa's house. But when I grew up, I moved 1,000 miles away, and it was difficult to find the time and money to visit often. Now that they're gone I regret not finding the time or money to make the trip. If I could do it over again, I'd take my four extra hours and help them grocery shop, clean their house, do yard work, or just sit and talk and talk and talk. Don't let precious time pass you by.

My Adventure: _____

_____

_____

Date: _____

5. Cook a meal (or meals).

If you have a friend or family member who's sick, just had a baby, is in the middle of finals, or mourning the loss of a loved one, take some of the day-to-day burdens off their weary shoulders and cook a meal (or meals) for them. Package them in freezer-friendly containers, and include reheating instructions.

My Adventure: _____

_____

_____

Date: _____

6. Clean the house of an ill friend.

If cooking isn't your thing (you don't want to make a sick friend sicker), offer to clean their house instead. It's alarming how quickly a house can go from neat-as-a-pin to natural disaster, especially if they have children. Help them recover by taking away the stress of looking at a cluttered or dirty space.

My Adventure: _____

_____

_____

Date: _____

7. Take your kids on an outing.

More than stuff and things, your kids want to spend time with you. Making memories from experiences and outings will last far longer than memories of the newest electronic toy. Take your four extra hours and make some magical memories that will last your kids a lifetime.

My Adventure: _____

_____

_____

Date: _____

8. Have a family/friend game night.

Board games have been relegated to the top shelf of the closet as lives get busier and electronic toys and social media have begun to monopolize our attention. But what a shame. Game nights are a way to connect with friends or family face-to-face. So resurrect the game night of yesteryear and have a little old-school board game fun.

My Adventure: _____

_____

_____

Date: _____

9. Drive an elderly relative to run errands.

Driving is something most of us take for granted. But age and injury can take away that ability. When that happens, what do we do? How do we get to the store? The doctor? The vet? It's scary when we feel trapped and lose independence. Ease the mind of an elderly relative or neighbor and offer to drive them on their errands. And while you do, make a point to talk to them. I'm sure they have some very interesting stories to tell.

My Adventure: _____

_____

_____

Date: _____

10. Be the friend you want to have.

Our lives move at warp speed and it's hard to slow down and share ourselves with others. But the act of caring and giving of yourself is vital for our own wellbeing, as well as that of our community. Start by being the friend you want to have. Take the time to talk with a friend. And more importantly, listen with an open heart. We are bombarded with noise every minute of every day. Sometimes the greatest gift is the gift of simply listening.

My Adventure: _____

_____

_____

Date: _____

17

TIME SAVING TIP #11

Divide and conquer!

Children aren't always given the credit they deserve for being able to handle chores on their own. No, really...don't laugh.

I have friends who have three children. Both parents are busy professionals with full-time jobs, and the kids are involved in all the usual Jr. High and High School activities. Yet they still seem to find time to spend together, do their homework, eat dinner together several times a week, and keep their house clean. When I first met them, I speculated at their secret. House elves? Time machine? Super-hero powers?

Then I spent a weekend at their house, and learned how they do it. Their family – and I mean every member –

shares the housekeeping chores equally. It was an amazing sight to see. I was so impressed, I had to ask my friend to share her secret to success.

Here's her secret: she *expected* her children to help, and then held them accountable. Shocking, huh?

Their philosophy was that every member of the family was a contributing member of the household. *Contributing* is the key word here. The kids weren't assigned chores in exchange for an allowance. Household tasks weren't treated as a "favor" kids did to help their parents. The running of the household was considered a shared responsibility.

From the age of about nine, she taught each child how to do laundry: sorting colors, washer/dryer settings, soap & softener – the whole bit. Once they got the hang of it, each child's laundry became their own responsibility. Sure, they had some parental oversight for a bit – but the bulk of the task fell to each child. And they were also held accountable if they didn't do it. If they didn't do their laundry, they had no clean clothes to wear. Period.

Sure, there were the occasional loads of whites-turned-pink. Kids sometimes went to school wearing dirty or wrinkled clothing. And she had to learn to let go and be OK with that. But it didn't take long before they learned that laundry was no joke. They still need prompting and reminders to do it once in a while. But it eventually gets done. And not having to do the entire household's laundry has freed up several hours a week for her.

They also have a similar system for doing dishes, and

other household chores. The best part of this system is that it not only saves her time and stress each week, it also teaches the children valuable life skills. Doing laundry and dishes are the obvious skills. But along the way they're also learning responsibility and accountability, planning ahead, scheduling and time management, the value of clothes, and the importance of caring for their belongings.

If you have kids, give it a try. It will probably be very frustrating at first, and feel like you're trying to push a boulder uphill. I know a lot of parents who give up and do all the chores themselves because they feel it's easier to just do it than to battle with their kids. But stay strong and stick with it. Before you know it you'll be enjoying a little more time to do all those things on your someday list.

18

TIME SAVING TIP #12

Measure your time!

Let's borrow a page from the corporate office playbook and apply some of their business tactics and strategies to our personal life. Here's a biggie: What gets measured gets done.

Simply put, if you set goals, put metrics (or measurable actions and results) around those goals, and hold yourself accountable, your goals will be met. But why do metrics make a difference? Easy. Metrics give us something concrete to work towards, and keep us focused on the task.

But there are tricks to making it work, and specificity is the key. For example, establishing some nebulous goal, like, "I want to have more time so I can do more stuff," does not give you defined parameters, actionable steps, or a measureable result to work towards. It's too wishy-washy to be anything more than a throw-away whine. Instead, say, "I would like to save 30 minutes each night in my mealtime prep so I can practice my guitar an extra 30 minutes a day."

Here's how it works. Let's use the meal-prep/guitar-practice scenario as an example.

First, establish a goal. Our goal is to shave 30 minutes off mealtime prep each night.

Second, know your starting point. In order to know where you need to go, you need to know where you are. So, measure (or estimate) how much time you're currently spending on meal preparation. (If you've implemented Time Saving Tip #1, you should already know this number.) This could include time spent grocery shopping after work, cutting veggies, assembling a casserole, etc.

Third, determine if your goal is feasible. If, in the second step, you find you're only spending 30 minutes a night preparing a meal, you know your goal of saving 30 minutes is probably not realistic. So, you either need to re-evaluate your starting point, or re-evaluate your goal.

Fourth, establish a game plan. Figure out where you can save time, and then do it. If you find you're spending 45 minutes at the grocery store after work each day, consolidate that time to one big shopping trip on Sunday afternoon. If you find you spend more time chopping veggies or mixing a casserole, try some slow-cooker meals, or buy pre-cut veggies. Not spending time going to the market or prepping produce means you have more time to practice your guitar.

Fifth, measure again. Measure how much time you spend prepping for meals, and see how much time you've saved. If you've saved, or "created," your extra 30 minutes, congratulations! If not, go back to steps one and two and see where you can readjust to find your 30 minutes.

CAUTION: Here's where you need to be intentional. Now that you've created the time to practice your guitar, you must actually practice your guitar. Otherwise, your efforts will have been for naught. Resist the urge to slump onto the couch and watch mindless TV. You must do something that is on your to-do list – something that is worth the time you're exchanging for it.

It's time to live proactively, not reactively. Your life is what you make it, so make it count.

Jennifer Lynn O'Hara

19

BONUS: ADVENTURE!

There is nothing quite like an adventure-driven adrenaline rush! Unfortunately, the fun-loving, adrenaline-pumping playtime activities are often relegated to the "when I have time" column on most people's to-do list.

Well, it's time to move those some-days to the top of your list, because today is the day! You're not getting any younger, and it's about time you start having the kind of "wow" experiences now that give you unbelievable stories to bore your grandchildren with later.

1. Ziplining.

Ziplining is an adrenaline trend that doesn't seem to be going anywhere anytime soon. Most cities and vacation spots have at least one ziplining opportunity, and usually multiple. It's a fun adrenaline rush. And the best part is that everyone looks equally ridiculous doing it.

My Adventure: _____

_____

_____

Date: _____

2. Escape Room.

Gather a group of friends and sign up to do an escape room. Experiences range from family-friendly to horror movie scary. If you've never heard of an escape room, here are the basics: You and your group are placed in a locked room and given a certain amount of time to escape from it. In the room is a basic clue or two, and solving each clue gets you your next clue, and one step closer to escape. If you like interactive brain games, an escape room might be just the thing for you. Hint: This is also a good team-building exercise for coworkers.

My Adventure: _____

_____

_____

Date: _____

3. Sky Diving.

I would never, *ever*, jump out of a perfectly good airplane. But far be it from me to keep someone else from doing it. I have friends who love it, and I am more than happy to photograph them on their way down. (Hopefully with an open and fully functioning parachute strapped to their back.) Beginners start with plenty of training. And the first few jumps are "tandem," where student jumpers are securely attached to their instructors.

My Adventure: _____

_____

_____

Date: _____

4. Bungee Jumping.

Adrenaline junkies and lovers of adventure flock to bungee jumping hot-spots. The sport is no longer limited to cranes at the county fair. Now you can strap a rubberband to your ankles and jump off of bridges, buildings, and even giant trees.

My Adventure: _____

_____

_____

Date: _____

5. Try weird food.

Take a food adventure. Research interesting and unusual food spots in your area and give them a try. Focus on ethnic foods you normally wouldn't eat. On a recent cruise, my mother tried frog legs, escargot, goat, and other exotic food offerings not normally found at your corner diner. If you're not as adventurous as my mom, start small. Try a Monte Cristo sandwich, sushi, or another mainstream food that's just outside your comfort zone. Keep pushing those culinary limits and expand your palate.

My Adventure: _____

_____

_____

Date: _____

6. Rappelling.

Rappelling looks like so much fun! And, you're attached by a rope, so the danger is mitigated. There are outdoor adventure companies that specialize in rappelling. Many outfitters combine hiking, camping, and rappelling in an all-inclusive adventure weekend. How fun does that sound?!

My Adventure: _____

_____

_____

Date: _____

7. 4-wheeling.

Have you ever seen Jeeps and pick-ups driving through town covered stem to stern in mud, and think, "What in the world did they just do to get that way?" The answer: 4-wheeling. Not all 4-wheel adventures include fun in the mud. But even mudless 4-wheeling is fun 4-wheeling. Go with a group that specializes in these types of adventures, so if something unexpected happens, you'll have a pro nearby to help.

My Adventure: _____

_____

_____

Date: _____

8. Parasailing.

Parasailing looks scary, but it's really quite peaceful. Once the initial lift-off is over, the rest of the ride is quiet and reflective – even reverent. The only thing you hear is the wind in your hair as you float through the air. And if something bad happens, you already have a parachute attached to your back, so you're good to go.

My Adventure: _____

_____

_____

Date: _____

9. Hot air ballooning.

Take a cue from The Wizard, or Jules Verne, and explore your corner of the world from the basket of a hot air balloon. The experience is exhilarating and peaceful at the same time. The idea of being suspended by hot air can be a bit disconcerting. But that worry is soon forgotten when you peer over the edge of the basket and marvel at the landscape passing peacefully below.

My Adventure: _____

_____

_____

Date: _____

20

TIME'S UP!

The moral of the story is this: Time is your most valuable asset. Don't waste it. You don't need to be a millionaire to improve your quality of life. A few simple lifestyle changes can help you find that elusive "extra time" you've been looking for. The trick is to determine what time-saving tips work for you (whether they're the ones in this book or your own) and make them a habit. You must be intentional about how you spend your time. Remember, whatever you trade for your time must be worth the cost.

Don't wait until the time is right. There will never be a perfect time to do something or to start something. Life has a habit of getting in the way of our plans, so if you wait, you'll miss it. You must make up your mind to do it regardless of the noise that distracts us. Ultimately, the choice is yours.

Avoid falling into the pit of excuses. There are a million of them! This book has been all about the "I don't have time" excuse. But there are so many others: I'm not good/talented/pretty/skinny/whatever enough, no one will help me, it's already been done, it's too late, I'm too old, I don't have the money, I don't have any motivation, I'm afraid to fail, and the list goes on and on.

I exhort you to throw those excuses out the window. Life is too short to let fear and insecurities, and the excuses they breed, keep us from living the most fulfilling and meaningful lives we can.

One of my favorite quotes goes something like this...

"Do not come to the end of your life only to find that you have not lived. Many come to the point of leaving the earth and when they gaze back, they see the joy and beauty that could not be theirs because of the fears they lived." — Clearwater

My prayer for you is that you live richly and fully, that you find the time to experience all the beauty and joy this life has to offer, and that when you reach the end of your time on this planet – a long, long, long, long time from now – you will be able to look back with no regrets.

God bless.

ABOUT THE AUTHOR

Jennifer Lynn O'Hara is a busy actress, singer, musician, artist, photographer, and author. She has appeared in numerous television and film projects and a multitude of stage productions, is a published poet and author, and has had her art shown in several exhibits. She is the regular host of the series, *A Single Girl's Guide To...*, and is an avid DIY-er and recipe creator.

Jennifer lives by the beach in Southern California with her two cats.

Follow Jennifer at twitter.com/alifeonthestage and via the travel, cooking, and lifestyle website asinglegirlsguideto.com.

www.ingramcontent.com/pod-product-compliance
Lightning Source LLC
LaVergne TN
LVHW051303080426
835509LV00020B/3134